The Political Economy of Fiscal Limits

The Political Economy of Fiscal Limits

John J. Kirlin
University of Southern California

LexingtonBooks
D.C. Heath and Company
Lexington, Massachusetts
Toronto

Library of Congress Cataloging in Publication Data

Kirlin, John J.
 The political economy of fiscal limits.

 Bibliography: p.
 Includes index.
 1. Tax and expenditure limitations—United States. 2. Real property tax—
California. 3. Local finance—California. I. Title.

HJ2051.K54	336.3'9'0973	79–3180
ISBN 0–669–03390–1		AACR2

Copyright © 1982 by D.C. Heath and Company

Published simultaneously in Canada

Printed in the United States of America

International Standard Book Number: 0–669–03390–1

Library of Congress Catalog Card Number: 79–3180

To my parents
Hazel R. and John C. Kirlin

Contents

List of Figures
and Tables

Acknowledgments

Almost two years before Proposition 13 was passed, conversations with local government officials whetted my interest in strains on the California intergovernmental fiscal system. Since then, conversations with California state and local officials have sustained that interest, provided new insights, and been a testing ground for my understanding of Proposition 13 and related events. Students in several classes heard my evolving thoughts on the issues explored in this volume; their questions and observations added to my understanding of this complex subject.

At various times, my research on Proposition 13 was supported by the John Randolph and Dora Haynes Foundation, the Lincoln Institute of Land Policy, and the United States Department of Housing and Urban Development. This support is gratefully acknowledged.

Scattered portions of chapters 3, 4, and 5 appeared under the title "Accommodating Discontinuity: Adjusting the Political System of California to Proposition 13," published in *Fiscal Stress and Public Policy,* C. Levine and I. Rubin, editors (Sage Yearbooks on Politics and Public Policy, vol. 9, copyright 1980, pp. 69–88), and is reprinted by permission of the publisher, Sage Publications (Beverly Hills/London).

Jillian McKillop and Thea O'Connell cheerfully typed the manuscript, often bending their schedules to fit my erratic progress. Mike McCarroll, Carolyn Yoder, and Susan Lasser of Lexington Books tolerated my tardiness in completing the manuscript. It is a different and, I believe, better book for having been delayed.

Finally, I must thank my wife Anne and daughters Kristin and Heather, without whose support and sustenance this book could not have been completed.

1 A Political-Economy Perspective on Fiscal Constraints

Proposition 13, approved by California voters by a two-to-one margin on June 6, 1978, focused national attention on the movement to limit government finances. Through the mid-1970s such a goal appeared to be held only by ideological conservatives and assorted eccentrics. The success of Proposition 13 (the Jarvis-Gann Initiative) precipitated a national political debate on fiscal limits. Similar measures were put before the electorate in several states; Howard Jarvis visited the nation's capital, where members of the House and Senate competed to be photographed with him, to guide him around Capitol Hill, to somehow be associated with the movement for fiscal limits.

Since that shock to the nation's political rhetoric, arguments have raged over the meaning of Proposition 13, over its strength and staying power, and over what impact it will have upon the operations of government, the services received by citizens, and the economy. It was soon recognized that Proposition 13 was not the initial evidence of an urge toward fiscal limits; other states and localities had adopted one or another variant of fiscal limits in the previous few years. Moreover, Proposition 13, and most of the thirty fiscal limits enacted in the 1970s, arrived after the expansion of the public sector had slowed (Pascal et. al. 1979; Shannon 1981). Although Proposition 13 was not the first event in what was soon named the Fiscal Limits Movement, the support of two-thirds of those voting in the nations's most populous and wealthy state had a cathartic political effect not unlike Caesar's crossing of the Rubicon or the Minutemen's ambush of British soldiers at Concord bridge. The issue of fiscal limitation was placed firmly on the public-policy agenda.

Despite the hopes of those alarmed by the Fiscal Limits Movement, the appeal of Proposition 13 has not disappeared in the years since its passage. Occasional surveys reveal Californians remain favorable toward the initiative. Moreover, other states and local governments have adopted fiscal limits measures, and President Reagan has successfully cut the federal budget and taxes. A fundamental restructuring of American politics may be under way. Certainly, the elements for such a restructuring exist: attitudes and behaviors of the electorate are changing, elected officials are seeking to cope with new issues, and relationships among units of government are

1

being affected as their respective revenue bases and expenditure abilities are altered.

One prognosis for the movement toward fiscal constraint is that it will fail. Failure could be obvious, as would occur if candidates favoring fiscal limits were consistently defeated, or if the electorate approved substantial tax increases. Failure could also take the form of the erosion of victory, if the policies and institutional changes advocated by supporters of the Fiscal Limits Movement were adopted but then evaded or subverted by interests with greater staying power in the ongoing political process, a familiar occurrence in American politics (Huntington 1952; McConnell 1966).

But to talk of success or failure, or of impact, requires criteria by which such judgments might be reached. Abraham Kaplan considers theory a way of making sense out of a disturbing situation. This process of understanding occurs largely by placing a new phenomenon in relationship to previous images and habits, changing those images and habits as needed (1963, p. 295).

This is an apt definition for the present case: some sense must be made out of the present shrinking of the public purse in terms of its place in the context of familiar events and understandings of the situation so that appropriate responses may be developed. If this fiscal limitation is seen as a temporary aberration, the appropriate response is to await the return of normalcy. If it is seen as an attempt to place issues on the political agenda (such as property-tax reform) without challenge to underlying processes, the appropriate response may be to calculate the balance of affected interests. If it is seen as an attempt to alter the balance of political power and control between a coalition of interest groups, elected officials, and public bureaucracies versus taxpayers in general, the appropriate response may be to calculate not only the balance of affected interests but also to seek resolution of the power conflict.

This analysis is based on a particular way of seeing the movement toward fiscal constraint. In broad terms, what is occurring may be characterized as a social experiment to impose more effective constraints on the proportion of the nation's annual product that passes through the public sector, and to reestablish the relevance of the mechanisms of political participation available to citizens. This perspective (to be developed further) considers efforts to impose fiscal constraint to be a response to fundamental frailties in the politics of the nation.

The Political-Economy Perspective

Any analyst is constrained by a perspective that guides attention to certain phenomena and provides a language and concepts through which understanding is developed and communicated. Such is the nature of analysis, and whether one calls these tools theories, frameworks, or perspectives, the fact that they shape perception and action and are but imperfect reconstructions of reality encourages recognition of the partiality of any insight.

These statements are unremarkable. Analysts frequently state and defend their approaches at the outset of analysis. Exploration of alternative frameworks is particularly important here, however, for the choice of perspective not only indicates the tools of analysis, but also delimits the phenomenon under study. In some areas of study, for example juvenile delinquency, or capitalization effects of taxes, or social stratification, a history of analysis has delimited the subject matter so that discussion may proceed with a relatively high degree of closure concerning which phenomena are relevant.

But what is a Fiscal Limits Movement? What are the possible impacts of fiscal constraint? By what standards shall these phenomena be evaluated? An attendee at any of the numerous conferences, workshops, or panels held concerning fiscal limits since passage of Proposition 13 could easily conclude that the definition employed by discussants reflected more the linkage they were able to make with concepts and theories already extant in their discipline than with any attributes of the phenomenon. And participants in political discussions usually interpret the movement through their preexisting ideological frameworks and expect impacts relevant to their knowledge base and interests. Again, this is to be expected; understanding is achieved most easily by relating that which is perceived as new to already-established constructs. And I certainly bring my existing intellectual tools to this analysis.

Yet, more than the usual degree of explicit attention to theoretical perspectives is desirable. In the first place, careful attention to alternative perspectives will help the community of analysts and social scientists map out the boundaries of the phenomenon under study and discover what disciplines may contribute to its understanding. More importantly, fiscal constraint is compelling critical public-policy choice making. Many public problems that generate pressure for public policymaking reach the political agenda at a particular point in time, but there is little other than media attention and interest-group pressure to compel choice making at that time. Even poverty or a crisis in health care are in such a category in this nation. Some issues are more critical because they challenge more fundamentally the fabric of our society. Civil rights in the mid-1960s was such an issue; energy and the economy became critical issues in the mid-1970s and remain so today; and I will argue that the constraint now being placed on the public sector is also a critical issue.

To label an issue critical is not to suggest that it will, or can, be resolved with a spasm of crisis-dominated public-policy choice making. The important distinguishing characteristic of these issues is that the direction established by the major responsive policy choices is critical to the nature of our society. Had repression instead of accommodation been the response to the mobilization of blacks in the 1950s and 1960s, American society would be far different today. If we continue as profligate energy consumers, we run a substantial risk to our economy and social fabric. If economic performance is not improved nor inflation curbed, our aspirations for economic progress and security will be dashed and the real economic situation of American citizens might well decline. Similarly, inappropriate policy responses to fiscal constraint, if the analysis of its causes presented herein is correct, could critically affect American society.

Indeed, a central theme of this book is that the responses to fiscal constraint will have greater impact on the nation than the loss of public-sector revenues or the reductions in expenditures and services that will be the immediately visible consequences of fiscal constraint. This will be the case whether fiscal constraint is the consequence of a fiscal limit such as Proposition 13, of federal tax and budget cuts, or of the accretion of numerous smaller actions to constrain public revenues now being taken by governments at all levels. Because the movement toward fiscal constraint is so strong, it will reduce the share of the Gross National Product that goes to state and local governments, for example, and the impact upon expenditures and services will be extensive. The responses generated will also be extensive and they too will have impacts. These impacts will be on the political system itself, defining its capacity for future choice and action. For example, the analysis undertaken here of responses to the Jarvis-Gann Initiative concludes that the state, and especially the state legislature, has gained powers over local governments in California. Because of the responses to that initiative, local governments now have less political capacity, as well as less fiscal capacity, with which to shape the futures of their communities.

A political-economy perspective that looks for causes and consequences of phenomena such as fiscal constraint in both the economic and political sectors of society, is virtually required for analysis of the movement toward fiscal constraint. Such an approach is used here, with the analysis sometimes focusing on just political or just fiscal phenomena, but most frequently on the interaction of the two. The political-economy perspective also suggests that individuals and organizations will generally respond to the incentives and constraints they confront in ways they calculate will serve their interests and values. This analysis shares this expectation.

From the perspective of policymakers and citizens seeking to construct the society they desire, the levers of change are found in the political system. Whether for causes of fiscal constraint, for explanation of the responses elaborated, or for possible future alternatives, the emphasis must be on political institutions and policy strategies. Economic issues (such as a depression or inflation) may stimulate policymaking and present opportunities and constraints (for example, the rate of economic growth). But the economy does not itself present policy options. Instead, policymakers must devise policies and programs that seek to affect the economy in accordance with their objectives, such as real economic growth of the nation or the development of a particular sector of the economy such as steel or a region such as Appalachia. Policymakers may also seek to intervene in economic markets in pursuit of such particular objectives as requiring investor-owned utilities to offer loans for insulation of residences to their customers. Finally, policymakers may consciously refrain from intervening in market inter-actions, believing them to produce more efficient societal outcomes than is possible through public policymaking, or that the individual choice making expressed in markets is so valued as to prohibit interference. Societal choice making, including choices as to division between the public and private sec-tors, must occur in the political system. Because change occurs, as the result of previous policy decisions or changes in technology, for example, the long-term, sustained capacity of the political system to make choices and to act must be maintained. Ideally, that capacity is nurtured and developed.

Thus, the overarching criterion by which any political system must be judged is its sustained capacity to choose and to act. If that capacity is lost, the political system unravels and is replaced; if that capacity decays, the choices made for society are likely to be erroneous or so poorly implemented as to be ineffective. The capacity of a political system should not be measured by the percentage of a nation's product that the system directly controls, nor by the variety and extent of activities it undertakes. Instead, political-system capacity must be measured by the system's ability to learn and to adapt (this standard is discussed further in chapter 6).

Proposition 13 and the Fiscal Limits Movement are interesting, among other reasons, because of what they reveal about the capacity of contem-porary political institutions. The analysis undertaken in this volume sug-gests that the capacity of our political system to deal with the longer-term dynamics of liberal-interest-group politics such as increasing costs or the widening politicization of society, is limited. California's political system groped for a decade with the issue of tax reform, finally reducing itself to a paralysis that was only destroyed by the outside stimulus of the Jarvis-Gann Initiative.

If Proposition 13, other fiscal limits, and the general experience of fiscal constraint have challenged the old bias toward an expansive public sector, they have not ensured any sensible new policy directions. Yet, as I have argued, the policies developed in response to fiscal constraint are critically important, for they shape the sustained capacity of our political system to choose and to act. In California, where three calendar years and four budget cycles have passed since voter approval of Proposition 13, an opportunity is offered to examine how such responses were developed and to estimate their impact. This analysis is a primary focus of this book, receiving attention in chapters 4 and 5. The major findings include increased power for the state in relation to local governments, an ascendant role for the California legislature, and the effort of that body to fit policy responses to the Jarvis-Gann Initiative into already established procedures. These responses seem ill-suited to increasing the capacity of the California political system to choose and act.

To reiterate one of the themes of this book, the diminution of political capacity of the California political system that has occurred since June, 1978 is not attributable directly to Proposition 13. It is, rather, attributable to the policies elaborated in response to the initiative. Discerning the causes for those responses is critical to understanding what has happened in California since Proposition 13 and to extrapolating that experience into any generalized theory about what may occur throughout the nation in response to fiscal constraint. In California, several factors influenced response to Proposition 13. Some were institutional, long-term features of the political system of the state, such as the constitutional role of the state legislature and its adherence to the "reform" model. Others were immediately context-specific, such as the existence of the state surplus. Most critical of all, however, were the theories on which responsive policies were based and the language employed in policy discussion.

How language and theory affected policymaking before and after Proposition 13 is given frequent attention in this book. The strong impact of dominant theory and language is evident in the deliberations concerning taxes and local governments in both periods. Although language and theory did change somewhat as a consequence of Proposition 13, much remained virtually the same in 1981 as in 1975–1977. As an example, discussion of how the state should relate to elementary and secondary education was little changed, with the exception that somewhat less attention was given to school-expenditure equalization. Because the issue of how language, theory, and action interrelate is so critical to understanding processes by which responses to fiscal constraint are developed, separate attention is given to this topic in chapter 6.

Language and theory are critical to policy choice in a political system because they powerfully affect perceptions of what are problems, what their causes might be, and what responsive policies might be developed. One way to look at this is to view the political system as composed of four sectors:

electoral

fiscal

institutional/constitutional

policy strategy

The electoral sector consists of elections, the institutions associated with the electoral process (such as parties), the laws governing elections and party organization (such as those regarding open primaries), and the behavior and attitudes of the electorate regarding political efficacy or ideology. A great deal of political-science literature concerns the electoral sector, and much is known of its operation.

The fiscal sector consists of the revenue-generation and expenditure patterns of government. Again, a substantial body of literature, developed mainly by public-finance economists, is available for this sector.

The institutional/constitutional sector consists of the formal structures of governments. The numbers and types of local governments, the powers of executive, legislative, and judicial branches of government, and the distribution of power and responsibilities in the federal system would be included here. Enumerations of jurisdictions by type are available here, as is a fairly rich legacy of studies analyzing the operation of a particular type of political institution (for example, the council-manager form of municipal government), particular institutionally based processes (such as the federal budget process), or particular offices (as the presidency). Much of the literature regarding this sector is normative, advocating a particular institutional or constitutional arrangement. Moreover, relatively little is known of behaviors in the interstices of public organizations, a question of increased importance as more policies are developed and implemented not by single governmental entities but intergovernmentally. Similarly, relatively little is known of the frequency and operation of what must be hundreds of thousands of nontraditional governmental structures such as quasi-public corporations or intergovernmental bodies that contract for services.

Finally, the policy-strategy sector consists of the ideas dominant in a specific time and place concerning effective policies. To an extent, these ideas are related to perceived public problems. For example, weak economic performance stimulates interest in policy strategies that might provide remedy. Although perceived problems may stimulate attention, they do not determine which public-policy strategies are dominant. An example is available from the Depression era: both presidents Hoover and Roosevelt believed the faltering economy to be a problem but their policy strategies in response to the Depression differed. A more recent example can be seen in the presidential transition from Carter to Reagan. The Reagan administration favors policy strategies that reduce government intrusion into society. Even if different administrations pursue the same objectives, they will tend to do so with different policies. Understanding of this sector is spotty. Analyses of periods of substantial change in dominant policy strategy (such as the Progressive Era, or the Franklin Delano Roosevelt administration) are common. But theoretical knowledge of this sector remains quite undeveloped.

Of importance to the present analysis is how change occurs in the four political-system sectors. The first observation that can be made is that change in each sector tends to be cyclical; a period of ferment being followed by a period of relative stability. The cyclical nature of change is most obvious in the institutional/constitutional sector, in which waves of reforms have left structures that are largely identified with specific time periods. Second, change in the four sectors tends to be linked in time, in stimulus, and in theoretical base. As an example, Reagan was elected president during a period of change in the electoral sector (evidenced by declining trust in government) and in the fiscal sector (seen in the arrival of fiscal constraint). He proposed changes in the institutional/constitutional sector (returning revenue sources to the states) and used a set of policy strategies that differed from those of his predecessor. The common stimuli were weak economic performance and perceptions of ineffective, expensive government. The common theory is not fully articulated, nor shared by every citizen. But it is not inchoate either; the core concept is that reduced domestic government may be more effective and efficient, and dominate individuals less. The third, and final, observation about change in this simple four-sector model is that conscious policy-making is central to the change process. Moreover, such policy choice is based on some theory of what is going on in society and how to achieve public-policy objectives. The choice of a base theory is often explicit, as was certainly the case for the Progressives and the Reagan administration. Change often begins with changing policy strategies, which stimulates change in the institutional/constitutional and fiscal sectors, and finally in the electoral sector, where citizen attitudes and voting behavior provide evaluation and legitimation or rejection of the changes undertaken. On occasion, as in the case of Proposition 13 in California, change emerges from the electoral process. Even here, however, it may be said that theory and policy strategies played a role, because they influenced the writing of the Jarvis-Gann Initiative and the voters' evaluation of that measure. This is easily seen in a comparison of Proposition 13 and the rejected alternative on the same ballot, a comparison that is undertaken in chapter 3.

Alternative Explanations of the Fiscal Limits Movement

The possibility that fiscal constraints raise central, critical issues is not a consensus position. Alternative perspectives have been advanced, each based upon an explanation of the causes of the Fiscal Limits Movement, the most visible manifestation of the movement toward fiscal constraint before Ronald Reagan assumed office. Three such alternative explanations are examined.

Before passage of Proposition 13, and even for some months thereafter, a frequent explanation of support for fiscal constraint was that fiscal limits were aberrations. 'It was just those crazy Californians again,' seemed to be the attitude of some. More telling, however, was the posture of California's political establishment prior to passage of Proposition 13. The overwhelming majority of elected officials, the major corporations, and professional public administrators sought to convince the electorate that Proposition 13 was unworkable, destructive charlatanism. The underlying presumption and frequent lament was that if citizens only knew what a good job government was doing, they would not behave aberrantly by voting for Proposition 13. This explanation of the causes of voter support for Proposition 13 was behind the (now weakening) expectation of many California public officials that once the citizenry experienced the consequences of the initiative, they would come to their senses and pre-Jarvis normalcy would somehow be reestablished. For some commentators on the national political scene, the defeat of several of the fiscal-limit measures on state ballots after Proposition 13 demonstrated that the Fiscal Limits Movement was ephemeral. This perspective may still prove correct, but the weight of present evidence suggests that it is more likely to have been naive, underestimating the strength of the movement toward fiscal constraint. But officials in Massachusetts resurrected this approach after passage of Proposition 2-½, so it still has adherents.

A second common perspective reduces the Fiscal Limits Movement to familiar interest-group politics. Property-tax payers are said to be pursuing reductions in their tax burden (Levy 1979). Although a tax revolt in California (with well-above-average property taxes and total state and local taxes nearly the highest of all states prior to Proposition 13) tended to support this hypothesis, the evidence weakens as other states are analyzed. For example, the Advisory Commission on Intergovernmental Relations (ACIR) analyzed the thirteen states where there were tax or spending measures on the November, 1978 ballot (1979, p. 9). Only two of the thirteen (Arizona and Hawaii) were judged to be heavy-tax states, measuring state and local tax revenue as a percentage of state personal income. And only two (Michigan and Nebraska) made heavy use of the property tax. Also conflicting with this perspective is the fact that citizen-initiated action was necessary for the vast majority of fiscal limits. The political systems were, for some reason, unable to provide the tax relief desired by a large block of the electorate. Thus the interest-group perspective does not provide a full explanation of the movement toward fiscal constraint.

Other commentators interpret fiscal constraint as evidence of a swing toward conservatism among the electorate. A variant of this perspective argues that the impetus behind Proposition 13 and similar measures is anti-black or anti-poor. Available survey data does not support either of these positions. Strong support for an active government, including strong support for specific services well known to have high costs, such as health care, welfare, police services, or environmental protection is found consistently in citizen surveys (Citrin 1979).

An argument that the movement toward fiscal constraint represents a major challenge to the political patterns of the last two decades must be based upon an analysis of those patterns. More fully developed in chapter 2, the thesis may be stated simply. Since World War II, and especially since 1965, the political system of the United States has become greatly more complex and interdependent. Policymaking and implementation were largely taken over by single-focus interest groups who pursued their objectives at all levels of the intergovernmental system. This single-issue and "vertical" politics contrasted with the formal, traditional mechanisms of political participation in the nation, which are general and "horizontal," that is to say, jurisdictional rather than issue-based. The contest between these two political patterns proved unequal and the political relevance of jurisdictions and related mechanisms of political participation declined. Proposition 13 and other fiscal-limits measures provide the electorate with an opportunity to redefine politics, reestablishing the relevance of participation in jurisdictional politics and shifting the focus of conflict from specific programs and policies to general fiscal issues.

Within this general interpretation, specific contextual factors are very important. For example, the direct-initiative process eases the difficulties of citizen-initiated political proposals. Nine of the seventeen states with direct initiatives had fiscal-limit initiatives on the November, 1978 ballot. Chapter 3 analyzes the specific context within which Proposition 13 was passed, including features of California politics (a strong Progressive legacy, weak political parties, and highly professionalized and bureaucratized public agencies), the California housing market, and the state and local tax systems.

Analyzing the Impacts of Proposition 13 and the Future of Fiscal Constraint

Though all of the ultimate impacts of Proposition 13 have not yet occurred, analysis of its effects yields several important conclusions. Chapter 4 analyzes its impact on intergovernmental fiscal-system policymaking and service delivery, chapter 5 the impact on the political system of California, and chapter 6 explores alternative responses to fiscal limits.

Largely because the extraordinary state surplus allowed a "bail-out" of California local governments, service levels have not been dramatically affected. A much greater impact is observable in the intergovernmental fiscal system, in which the state has dramatically increased transfers to local governments, and the dilemmas posed in effectuating such transfers are well-illuminated. Second-order policy changes are beginning to emerge as local governments adjust to the new era. For example, uncertainty over future revenue sources and expenditure obligations is changing local governments' land-use policymaking. The impact on political systems is also slowly becoming apparent. A more-than-ordinary proportion of incumbent office-holders have been defeated. The language of policymaking has changed from that of expansion to that of constraint. Further limitation of state and local revenues and expenditures is occurring. Concerning the assertion of social control by the electorate, or of jurisdictional values over policy issues, the evidence is unclear. Proposition 13 certainly broke through the paralysis on tax reform that had been the state legislature's response to conflict among pressure groups. But greater centralization of political power at the state level may well make citizen access more difficult. And policy deliberations in the legislature over local government bail-outs have been heavily influenced by the same values and theories that were powerful before Proposition 13.

2

Frailties of American Political Institutions: Diversity, Interdependency, and Complexity

One approach to understanding Proposition 13 is to concentrate narrowly on the immediate context of its passage. Frank Levy (1979) employed this approach, analyzing the succession of tax-reform efforts that preceded Jarvis-Gann for evidence of why it passed after several earlier attempts had failed. Levy advanced increased property taxes as the primary cause, resulting from the application of statutory requirements that all property be assessed at 25 percent of market value in a period of escalating property prices, as well as several reinforcing features of the California context. He concluded that Proposition 13 was a vote to cut property taxes, and that any cuts in governmental spending were incidental consequences (1979, p. 86).

This interpretation is valid, but partial. The issues of increasing home values, a property-tax burden shifting increasingly to homeowners (versus commercial, industrial, and agricultural property owners), and a state legislature and governor unable to provide tax relief were immediately behind Levy's property-tax thesis. Levy explores these issues but with a different interpretation than in this analysis. But a broader circle of issues exists. Proposition 13 was not an isolated phenomenon; it was preceded and followed by other fiscal limits. Why did the issue of fiscal limitation arise in over half of the states at about the same time? Why has it often taken direct citizen action to force the issue onto the political agenda? These broader issues are considered in this chapter, and issues relevant specifically to the adoption of Proposition 13 in California are taken up in chapter 3.

In the context of these larger issues, Proposition 13 and the Fiscal Limits Movement achieve a more general meaning and provide insight into the dynamics of our political system over the last two decades. My central thesis has already been stated: policies and institutions developed in response to the advancing industrialization of our nation are issue-based, while the constitutional structure of our government and traditional mechanisms of political action are based in geographically defined jurisdictions. The conflict between these two types of political systems has not been resolved constitutionally, in the structures and powers of governmental institutions, nor has it been resolved in the political culture and practices of citizens. Instead, policies have been developed that seek to patch over the most troublesome contradictions, as in the case of increased fiscal transfers from state and federal to local government (Hamilton 1978a), a strategy that pursues more or less similar policies throughout the nation while maintaining the form at least of autonomous, geographically distinct governments.

Federalism Eroded: The Demise of a Constitutional Bias toward Jurisdictional Politics

The United States possesses the most fragmented and complex political system of any industrial nation. Division of political authority was the intent of the framers of the Constitution, who emphasized the separation of power between the executive, legislative, and judicial branches and between the states and the federal government, sowing the seeds of subsequent fragmentation.

As the nation expanded geographically and more states were created, there was a great increase in the number of local political jurisdictions, created in response to an urbanization that the original proponents of federalism could not foresee. Fragmentation of political authority does not necessarily beget complexity. As long as each jurisdiction is relatively autonomous, raises its own revenues and determines its own policies, the governmental system should not be characterized as complex. Complexity is more properly recognized as the consequence of interdependence among jurisdictions. Interdependence has encouraged development of governmental mechanisms that do not coincide with the geographical boundaries of general-purpose governments (such as cities) and/or have separate governing structures.

A major feature of this movement from simple federalism to an interdependent, intergovernmental system is the elaboration of structures beyond those of general-purpose governments. Nearly 22,000 general-purpose units of government exist in the United States according to the 1977 Census of Governments (1 national, 50 state, 3,062 county, and 18,862 municipal).

This governmental structure has been made complex by six responses to the demands of increasing industrialization, all amplifications of the underlying structure of general-purpose units of government.

First, an additional 57,000 units of government exist. Of these, a great number are townships (18,822). These may be seen as essentially within the original federal concept, since townships are largely minor subdivisions of counties, established almost as field offices, to perform limited functions such as road maintenance. Many additional units are school districts (15,175), which depart from the original image of a federal system in two regards: they are focused on a single activity, and they are often not coterminous with the boundaries of any other local government (often extending into unincorporated areas or across boundaries of more than one municipality, rarely encompassing all of a county). Special districts (25,962) are more clearly a response to the inadequacies of general-purpose governments in an urbanized industrial nation. These are created, often by general-purpose governments, to provide a single service to residents of an area. Special districts need not be coterminous with any other jurisdiction and may overlap one another or other jurisdictions. This flexibility has encouraged formation of special districts where problems do not conform to existing jurisdictional boundaries (in cases such as flood control, mosquito abatement, or water provision).

Second, local-government authority has been fragmented by the establishment of various public or quasi-public authorities, each with responsibility for undertaking a specific activity, and each governed under procedures separate from those of the existing jurisdiction, most frequently by a separate board. These authorities have been established in two historical periods. The earliest were established before World War II, largely under the impulse of progressive distrust of elected officials. These authorities commonly focused on development of infrastructure or provision of services (such as water) for which fees could be charged. The second group of authorities were established after World War II and mostly after 1965 to implement federal programs. These usually had a social purpose such as public housing or redevelopment.

Third, a wide variety of service-provision mechanisms have been developed that go beyond the organizational capabilities of any single jurisdiction. Those most commonly used by local governments are intergovernmental service-provision agreements, contractual provision of a service by a private firm, and governmental franchise of a private firm. Intergovernmental agreements include joint-service provision, joint construction and leasing agreements, agreements for loans of personnel or equipment, and contracts under which one governmental jurisdiction provides services to another (Zimmerman 1973). Private firms are most active in provision of refuse collection; a survey by Savas (1977) found that two-thirds of the sampled cities provided at least part of their refuse-collection services through private firms, either under contracts or franchises.

Fourth, grants-in-aid from the federal to state and local governments and from state to local governments increased. In Fiscal Year (FY) 1957, state transfers to local governments totaled $7.3 billion, nearly double the $3.9 billion in federal grants-in-aid to states and localities. State and federal fiscal transfers were nearly equal by FY 1974 ($45.6 and $43.3 billion respectively). Federal aid represented 10.1 percent of state and local expenditures in FY 1955, and by FY 1978, the height of federal grants-in-aid, it represented approximately a quarter of those expenditures. In virtually all cases, the increased grants-in-aid were designated for specific purposes, such as health-services planning, rather than general fiscal support.

Fifth, beyond the effects of regulations attached to grants-in-aid, federal and state governments have substantially narrowed the policymaking flexibility of local governments in the last fifteen years. Much of this narrowing of local discretion resulted from mandates of service provision upon local governments, most frequently by states (ACIR 1978; Lovell 1979; U.S. Office of Management and Budget (OMB) 1980; Lovell and Tobin 1981). Federal mandates have often taken the form of crosscutting regulations intended to direct the behavior of local governments by threatening denial of federal aid. These crosscutting regulations have been concentrated in the areas of environmental protection, civil rights, citizen participation, planning requirements, and prescribed management procedures (OMB 1980).

Sixth, substate, supralocal-government agencies have proliferated. By and large, these are the creations of the federal government, though some states have also generated these structures. Perhaps the most visible are the councils of government of which there is one in nearly every metropolitan area, promoted by the federal government. But functionally, specific substate units are much more frequent, such as Area Agencies on Aging and Health Systems Agencies. Many major federal programs operate through such agencies. An example of a state-substate regional agency is the California Coastal Commission.

Any description of the American political system, then, must recognize the extraordinary richness and complexity of interrelationships among its institutions. Moreover, dramatic changes in that system occurred in the 1960s and 1970s. During that period, the increases in complexity and interdependence led to political decision making that occurred less in traditional jurisdictions and more in the intergovernmental mechanisms and agencies developed. Virtually no public official is now solely responsible for any policy decision; all authority is intergovernmental. As a consequence, no citizen can hold any public official solely responsible for a policy, either desired or abhorred. The constitutional nesting of powers, in which states are superior to localities, and the federal government to states in most respects, is only a partial corrective to interdependence and complexity. In some areas, preemption by a superior government has established clear responsibility in that superior unit. But more frequently, states choose to act by influencing the behavior of local governments, and the federal government seeks to act by influencing the actions of states and localities. These relationships are partnerships, with no clear designation as to who has the ultimate responsibility for decision making, although the dynamics involved have led to a diminution of local discretion and an expansion of state, and particularly national, governmental powers (ACIR 1980).

Interest Groups: From Diversity Expressed
to Diversity Created

From its founding, the political system of the United States has been based on the assumption that diverse interests will contend for influence in the political system. Madison's Federalist Paper No. 10 is a treatise on how factions may be allowed to express their interests without dominating the political system. As the nation expanded geographically, grew economically, and received many immigrants, the diversity of interests multiplied.

American political parties have been largely coalitions of interest groups. Theodore Lowi has argued that not only have interest groups characterized the American political system, but also they have been elevated to a central role in our conception of democracy (1979). This occurred as the delegation of governmental authority to interest groups was defined as democracy (McConnell 1966).

If the longstanding pattern of American politics is based upon interest groups, is there anything new in the last two decades that has changed the texture of this interest-group-based system? Five interrelated but significantly different developments can be identified.

The first is the decline of political parties. Among the explanations offered for the decline of political parties are the movement to media-based campaigns, the waning attachment of the electorate to parties, and the inability of parties to discipline members once elected. Ladd (1978) has argued that the very reforms intended to open parties to wider participation have made it much more difficult for them to perform their traditional roles of assisting in selection of leaders and of representation.

The second factor is the rise of single-issue groups, especially those based on noneconomic issues. Earlier examples of such groups exist, and they were at times successful, as when temperance groups imposed prohibition on the country. But there are now many more such groups. Their importance to the electoral system is in the way in which they judge candidates and policies by a litmus-paper-type test of support or opposition for their position, and in their ability to provide financing for and expression of grass-roots sentiment on particular issues.

The third distinctive development is partially a consequence of the activities of the single-issue interest groups just mentioned, and partially a response to the increased complexity of an advanced industrial nation. Lilley and Miller (1977) characterize much of the policymaking of the last decades as increasing *social* regulation. This is contrasted with earlier policies emphasizing *economic* regulation. Social regulation is particularly important because it affects the federal system, leading to increased federal and state demands on local governments and substantially increasing interdependence in the political system.

Fourth, the public sector has become much larger, providing an expanded set of access points for interest groups. Moreover, the very size of the public sector has introduced new issues into the political system. For example, public employment is viewed as a way to help balance economic activity and to deal with the problems of those who have difficulty in finding employment in the nongovernmental sector. Public employment has been especially important for the mobility of Blacks, and very high percentages of middle-income Blacks are employed in the public sector (Erie 1980).

The consequences of interest-group-based politics for the intergovernmental system can be seen through adaptation of Olson's model of how interest groups develop in a democracy (1965). In a democratic system, more and more interest groups will organize as time passes. Since organizational costs are not insignificant, those groups with the strongest interests (usually economic) organize first. Increases in the capability of the media to inform individuals nationwide of issues, and the decreasing cost of personal transportation and communication, makes it easier for groups with weaker interests to organize. This is especially important for groups whose members are widely dispersed, such as environmentalists. Groups whose members are widely dispersed have incentive to focus on policymaking at more inclusive levels of government. They may then demand compliance with their policy objectives on lower levels and use courts and other mechanisms to strive for compliance in the private sector.

The consequences of interest-group politics are not only an expression of these interests, but a transformation of politics, as candidates become more dependent upon single-issue groups. The political system is transformed in at least two ways. First, the representational/broker role of political parties and officials is made more problematic as they find it ever more difficult to define any general interest. Second, single-issue politics abolishes distinctions among jurisdictions, leading to policymaking that affects governments throughout the intergovernmental system. In contrast, the earlier economically based interest groups did not greatly affect the entire intergovernmental system as they pursued their objectives. Rather, they sought advantage through specific new programs (such as soil conservation) or through tax advantages or regulations. In most cases these policy objectives were achieved through the adoption of policy by specific units of government and had only modest impact on other units in the intergovernmental system.

Finally, in a transformation to be more fully analyzed, members of Congress themselves become the source of policy initiation. After analyzing policymaking in seven functional areas, the Advisory Commission on Intergovernmental Relations (ACIR) (1980) concluded that individual members of Congress, acting as "public entrepreneurs," were the most frequent source of new policies. Table 2–1 reports this analysis. Policy initiation was the currency congressmen used to develop political support. In most of the cases analyzed by ACIR, policy formation preceded interest-group formation; indeed the former stimulated the latter. In all of the cases analyzed, impact on the intergovernmental system was evident, and the role of the national government was strengthened vis-à-vis states and local governments. Congress evolved from being the arena for interest-group conflict to being the creator of interest groups. This change helped individual members of Congress solve the problem of developing political support in an environment in which traditional political structures were in disarray, but they did so only by further weakening the bases of jurisdictional politics. This same dynamic will be evident in the analysis of how the California legislature responded to Proposition 13, in ways that ameliorated problems, but further weakened California local governments.

The Requirements of Advanced Industrialization: Joining of Economy and Polity

It is often argued that the United States has become an advanced industrial nation in the years since World War II (Bell 1974; Heilbroner 1975). The defining attributes of this stage of economic development are change in employment patterns and in the relative size of sectors of the economy (manufacturing, agriculture and resource extraction declining while services and government increase). The public sector expands as "welfare-state" functions such as health, education, and income-security grow in scope and benefit levels. The role of government vis-à-vis the economy also changes, from that of a "referee" (enforcing rules of appropriate marketplace interaction) to two new roles. The first new role is to remedy societal disruptions that are not handled by existing market interactions, such as unemployment, environmental degradation, or growth/recession cycles. Secondly, government itself increasingly assumes a planning-programming role, undertaking organization of the production and/or consumption of goods or services (Janowitz 1976; Lindberg et al. 1975). Additionally, of course, other new issues have caused an expansion of the governmental presence in society. Advancement of the interests of minorities and consumer-protection policies are two important examples.

Though state and local governments often made the initial policy inno-

Table 2–1
Major Actors and Forces in Policy Development and Growth

Type of Actor	*Functional Fields—ACIR Case Studies*						
	Public Assistance	*Elementary and Secondary Education*	*Higher Education*	*Environment*	*Unemployment*	*Libraries*	*Fire Protection*
Internal policy actors							
Congress	x	x	x	x	x	x	x
President		x			x		x[b]
Interest groups		x		x		x	x
Bureaucracy				x	x		
Courts		x		x			
External policy actors							
Public opinion	x[a]			x			
Elections							
Political parties					x		
Press	x[a]			x			
Environmental influences							
Demographic and social trends	x	x	x		x		
Dislocations (war, depression)	x	x	x				

Source: Advisory Commission on Intergovernmental Relations, *In Brief: The Federal Role in the Federal System: The Dynamics of Growth* (Washington, D.C.: Advisory Commission on Intergovernmental Relations, 1980).

[a]Food stamps only.

[b]Interest groups were crucial in the creation of the U.S. Fire Administration only.

vations in these areas, in time the national government assumed the dominant role. In part, the logic of the policies themselves impels the development of a national response. To say that every American is entitled to income security is a politically relevant statement, while to apply the same statement to every resident of Tupelo, Mississippi, or the state of New Jersey, has little political relevance. Only the national government has control of monetary and fiscal policies, so it must assume responsibility for managing the economy. Moreover, the federal government, because of its greater access to income taxes and debt issuance, has the larger, more flexible, and more elastic revenue base needed to finance an expanded public sector.

This change in the scope of federal-government policy has two attributes that are significant departures from previous political patterns in the nation. For one, in the last decade, managing the economy was *the* preeminent objective of national policy, often displacing foreign affairs, national defense, and domestic programs (insofar as they are intended to achieve certain objectives). Economic issues loomed larger in foreign affairs, defense expenditures fluctuated as much in response to the needs of economic policy as to those of national security, and expenditures on domestic programs expanded and contracted on an economic basis. Second, the intergovernmental system was transformed, and all levels of government became much more interdependent and stronger linkages developed among bureaucracies and programs at various levels that shared functions (for example, federal, state, local health-oriented agencies and programs).

Beer (1974; 1976) offers an insightful analysis of contemporary intergovernmental policies in which subnational governments act to influence national policies. He argues that this representational role was at the core of the theory of federalism used by framers of the Constitution. The public sector of the polity (defined as centers of influence within government itself, such as bureaucrats who act as policy advocates, executives who formulate budgets, or county officials who lobby state legislators), has become much more influential, according to Beer. Technocrats wield increased influence over functionally specific programs, while *topocrats,* that is, state and local officials, represent the interests of their geographically delimited jurisdictions before both executive and legislative branches of the federal government.

The expansion of public-sector political power initially took the form of increased influence of technocrats, to which Beer attributes the spectacular increase in the number of federal categorical grants-in-aid to state and local governments, which increased from 160 in the early 1960s to over 1,000 by the mid-1970s (1978, p. 18). Over time topocrats organized as intergovernmental lobbies (the U.S. Conference of Mayors, National Association of Counties, National League of Cities, and others), and pressed for a shift toward noncategorical aid (such as federal revenue sharing). Beer calculates that such aid accounted for a quarter of federal aid by 1975, compared to a miniscule 2 percent in 1966 (1978, p. 18). Though this shift occurred, Beer has probably overemphasized the power of the topocrats and underappreciated how preeminent economic policymaking became during this same period of time. For example, anticyclical-stimulus grants-in-aid exceeded General Revenue Sharing in the FY 1979 federal budget. What Beer has excluded from his analysis is the impact of beliefs concerning the proper role of government, and particularly the importance of economic theory as both a source of legitimacy and stimulus for policy.

Indeed, I have argued elsewhere (Kirlin 1979) that adjustments to accommodate the policy requirements of advanced industrialization had greatly affected the intergovernmental grants-in-aid system before the advent of general revenue sharing. Table 2–2 analyzes changes in federal grants-in-aid over the past decade and a half. In constant dollars, these outlays increased approximately sevenfold.

More important are the changes in the objectives of grants-in-aid. An initial appreciation of the change can be found by contrasting the language used to describe grants in *Government Finances in 1956* (U.S. Bureau of the Census 1957) with that used in *Special Analyses of the Budget of the United States, 1980* (OMB 1979). The earlier document defends budget cuts to balance the federal budget and describes grants targeted at very specific programs such as highways. By the end of the 1970s, federal expenditures were justified in terms of a full-employment budget and the number of program objectives had proliferated. The role of the federal government in management of the nation's economy had greatly expanded, at least in aspiration, even if the objective of sustained growth while controlling inflation appeared elusive.

The increased attention to management of the economy is seen in table 2–2 in the increased outlays for three offset functions, intended to smooth cycles of growth, to assist depressed regions or sectors of the economy, and to redress negative externalities. Also shown are outlays for welfare-state programs of health, education, and income security, and for General Revenue Sharing. Six fiscal years are shown: FY 1957, an Eisenhower-era baseline; FY 1967, a Great Society year in the presidency of Lyndon Johnson; FY 1971, the year prior to General Revenue Sharing, during the Nixon presidency; FY 1974, the trough of a recent recession; and FY 1979, the proposed budget for the year in which Proposition 13 was passed.

The shift to a more active management of the economy is evident. Outlays for welfare-state programs, about two-thirds of all grants-in-aid in FY 1957, peaked at 71 percent in 1971, and have by 1979 declined to little more than 50 percent. Part of this decline is attributable to the assumption by the federal government of direct provision of selected income-security

Table 2-2
Federal Grants-in-Aid to State and Local Governments
(millions of dollars)

Fiscal Year	Total Outlays		"Welfare State" Programs		Antistructural Distress		Anticyclical Distress		Redress Negative Externalities		General Revenue Sharing		Percentage of Total Outlays in These Five Categories
	Current Dollars	Constant Dollars (1972=100)	Current Dollars	Percentage of Total Outlays	Current Dollars	Percentage of Total Outlays	Current Dollars	Percentage of Total Outlays	Current Dollars	Percentage of Total Outlays	Current Dollars	Percentage of Total Outlays	
1979	85,020	49,373[a]	44,683	52.6	8,312	9.7	9,007	10.6	5,578	6.6	6,852	8.1	87.6
1977	68,396	46,496	38,209	55.9	6,913	10.1	4,714	6.9	4,189	6.1	6,758	9.9	88.9
1974	43,308	36,424	27,350	63.2	4,134	9.5	598	1.4	2,132	4.9	6,106	14.1	93.1
1971	28,102	29,745	20,037	71.3	4,157	14.8	—	—	739	2.6	—	—	88.7
1967	15,240	21,167	8,767	57.5	1,362	8.9	19	0.1	305	2.0	—	—	68.5
1957	3,873	7,471	2,517	65.0	114	2.9	—c	—	b	b	—	—	67.9

Sources: U.S. Office of Management and Budget, *Special Analysis of the Budget of the United States* for 1967–1979 data. (Washington, D.C.: Government Printing Office, 1979). FY 1957 data from: U.S., Bureau of the Census, *Summary of Governmental Finances in 1957* (Washington, D.C.: Government Printing Office, 1957).

aConstant dollars for FY 1979 estimated by extrapolation of 1973–1977 inflation rate on state and local purchases (8.2%).

bData not available.

programs previously provided by state and local governments with federal assistance (Hamilton and Rabinovitz 1977). The percentage of total federal grants-in-aid represented by these five categories increased from about two-thirds in the 1957–1967 decade to about 90 percent since 1971. Even before General Revenue Sharing, then, the composition of federal grants-in-aid shifted toward outlays congruent with an advanced industrial economy. Because total outlays were increasing rapidly during this period, the shifts to new objectives did not require a dollar-for-dollar reduction in previous expenditures, but there was a notable reduction in grants-in-aid for high-ways.

   This transformation of federal grants-in-aid occurred in three stages. In the first, between 1965 and 1971, grants in support of health, education, and income-security programs, and of programs focused upon structural distress, increased as a part of the Great Society. For example, urban renewal and Model Cities programs expanded, as did outlays for economic assistance and manpower training. The second phase, from 1972 to 1975, was initiated by the arrival of General Revenue Sharing and the movement to block grants (such as the Community Development Block Grant program which replaced earlier urban renewal and Model Cities programs in the Department of Housing and Urban Development) was an impulse that waned rapidly, although the formula-allocation features of block grants often persisted. The third phase was marked by the rapid growth in anti-cyclical programs (for example, the temporary employment programs in the Comprehensive Training and Employment Act (CETA), Public-Works Employment, Job Opportunities, and Anti-Recession Fiscal Assistance) intended to stimulate the economy to counteract the recession of 1974, but that did not entail significant outlays until FY 1975, and peaked in FY 1979. During this period, of course, the economy was recovering, so these programs not only missed their stated objective, but probably contributed to inflationary pressures that characterized the period. Another feature of the third phase was the growth of grants to redress negative externalities, the largest portion of which (nearly $5 billion in FY 1979) supported construction of sewage-treatment plants.

   Domestic-policy inititives undertaken by President Carter may be understood as a continuation and institutionalization of management of the economy as the preeminent policy objective of the federal government. The debates concerning national urban policy, renewal of the CETA, and discussions of the future of General Revenue Sharing were all framed in terms best understood from this perspective.

   Although the Urban Growth and New Community Development Act of 1970 committed the federal government to policies intended to counteract economic distress in urban America, only under President Carter did this objective move to the forefront of urban policy. Carter's urban policy, announced on March 27, 1978, fully embraced the primacy of economic objectives. A new series of job, tax-incentive, grant, loan, and public-works efforts, plus redirection of existing federal programs, was aimed at improving the economies of distressed cities and regions, a clear departure from policies of the Nixon-Ford era and also from Carter's early policies.

As noted, the initial Nixon-Ford initiatives sought to enhance the general capacity of state and local governments to meet problems (through General Revenue Sharing, and community-development and law-enforcement block grants). In response to the recession of 1974, major initiatives were launched to combat unemployment: appropriations to CETA Temporary Employment, Public-Works Employment, Job Opportunities, and Anti-Recession Fiscal Assistance grew to nearly $5 billion in FY 1977.

Carter's initial policies accelerated policies focused on unemployment, projecting an expenditure of $9 billion in this area for FY 1979. As inflation replaced unemployment as the primary focus of national policymaking, CETA Temporary-Employment appropriations dropped, and Anti-Recession Fiscal Assistance and Public-Works Employment atrophied. But the emphasis on economic issues remained, and the debate focused on the extent to which aid should be directed to distressed areas. Conflict became regional, the debate over changing the formula for allocation of Community Development Block Grant funds pitting the northern "Frostbelt" against the southern "Sunbelt" (Havermann and Stanfield 1977).

Although much of the congressional rhetoric concerning CETA renewal and appropriations (1978–1979) focused on fraud and misuse of funds, the basic shift of concern from unemployment and stimulation of the economy to concern for inflation was much more critical to the ultimate size and form of the program. By reducing the appropriations and sharply restricting eligibility to long-term, hard-core unemployed, Congress clearly recognized the shift from the objective of countering a general recession to that of fighting inflation while seeking to assist the unemployed. Moreover, renewal of General Renevue Sharing was in jeopardy as concern over inflation and pressure to reduce the federal deficit mounted. Nothing is remarkable about these policy debates from the perspective focusing on management of the national economy.

The primary objectives of national domestic policies have changed, and caused changes in the fiscal flows that provide the framework for the intergovernmental system of the nation. Many important interest groups are threatened by this change in policy premises and seek to advance alternatives. State and local governments push for continuation of General Revenue Sharing, for example. And advocates of the poor argue that they are being sacrificed in the shift to a politics of economic management. Despite these counterforces, it is unlikely that the preeminence of the goal of managing the economy will be successfully challenged. Indeed, the United States has not yet moved as far in this direction as have other advanced industrial-ized nations (D. Cameron 1978). This trend does not mean, of course, that other policy objectives such as aid to the disadvantaged will be abandoned, only that these objectives must also find justification within the framework of economic-management policies. The most important consequences of this accommodation are likely to be greater volatility in funding levels and a continued debate over policies aimed at general economic performance versus policies targeted at specific groups of individuals, regions, or sectors of the economy. Even when the objectives of domestic policy include a large amount of presidential reelection politics, much policymaking fits within this rubric. For example, the 1979 payments to the poor to defray higher energy costs can be viewed as an offset policy, intended to assist a category of individuals disadvantaged by increased energy costs. And congressional reconsideration of antirecessionary aid in late 1979 and early 1980, appar-ently stimulated by Congressman Brooks' interest in reelecting Jimmy Carter, revived debates on how to disburse aid among areas experiencing economic difficulties.

However, because of the antistatist legacy of our political culture, the public sector may never assume the dominant role in the economy that it has in other advanced industrialized nations. The election of Ronald Reagan to the presidency in 1980, the gains of Republicans in the Senate in that election, and the success of Reagan in development of the FY 1981–1982 budget provide clear evidence of the strength of the antistatist sentiment in the electorate. Reagan even proposed reversing the growth of the role of the national government in the nation's economic and political systems.

It is important to recognize that the motivations and justifying logic of this approach involve more than old-style conservative opposition to expan-sive government. The economic theory that provided both impetus and rationale for the expansion of the policymaking scope of the national government is also under challenge. As doubt grew concerning the ade-quacy of Keynesian economic theory, and was reinforced by the evident in-ability of policies based on this theory to ameliorate the "stagflation" that gripped the nation's economy in the late 1970s, the search for an alternative economic theory intensified (Bosworth 1980). Supply-side economics was proffered by some as the new theory, but has not achieved domination of the policy process. Until policymakers again reach consensus on an eco-nomic theory, national policymaking will be unstable and shifting.

**Strain in the American Political System: Political
Institutions and the Rise of Fiscal Limits**

In the first chapter, a four-sector model of the American political system was developed. The analysis presented to this point in this chapter have emphasized three of the sectors: the fiscal, institutional, and policy-strategy dimensions of our political system. Substantial changes in each occurred in the 1960s and 1970s. Governmental fiscal systems changed from systems in which jurisdictions raised and expanded funds as individual units, into an intergovernmental fiscal system in which the transfer of funds among jurisdictions is pervasive. New policies were elaborated, often in response to new ideas concerning the role of the national government in managing the nation's economy. By the end of the 1970s the overwhelming proportion of federal grants-in-aid to state and local governments, and many of the non-fiscal federal policies directed at states and localities (such as regulations and mandates) could be explained in terms of theories concerning the role of the federal government in the nation's economy. Not surprisingly, these developments in the intergovernmental fiscal system and in policy strategies affected governmental and political institutions throughout the nation. New governmental units were created at all levels. But the most important impacts in the political sector were the increases in functional fragmentation and interdependence among institutions, and the decline in the relevance of jurisdictional politics and the traditional (party) institutions associated with it.

As suggested in the initial presentation of the four-sector model, change in one sector stimulates change in the others. Changes in the magnitude of three sectors in the 1960s and 1970s would be expected to stimulate change in the remaining sector, that of electoral politics. An analysis is now undertaken to determine what changes ultimately occurred, and their relationship to fiscal limits.

Figure 2-1 reports citizen attitudes toward government and taxes, and voting rates in national elections in the years preceding pasage of Proposition 13. The decline in citizen approval of government is striking. Although many individuals attribute this decline to Watergate and the Vietnam War, as then-president Carter did in his July, 1979 speech exhorting the nation to meet the energy crisis, the roots of disaffection are deeper than those two events.

Three measures of citizen distrust in government are shown. Two have nothing to do with Watergate or the Vietnam War. When asked if government wastes a lot of money, the percentage of survey respondents who responded affirmatively increased by over one-third between 1965 and 1978. The increase in the percentage of survey respondents who believed that public officials don't care what people think increased even more dramatically, nearly doubling between 1965 and 1973. The general measure of trust in government fell precipitously, at least partially because of Watergate and the Vietnam War. During the same period, voter participation in elections declined. Voting in elections for the U.S. House of Representatives went down nearly one-fifth in fifteen years.

The fiscal bases of citizen concern are shown by two measures. The per-

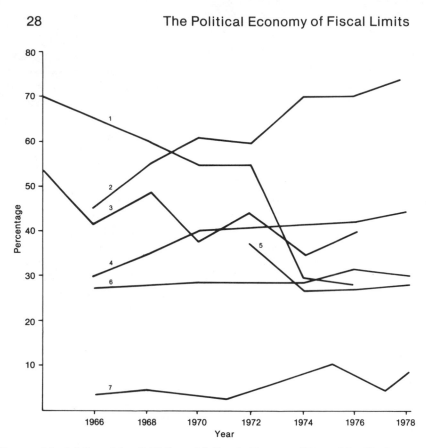

Source: Adapted from John. J. Kirlin and Jeffrey I. Chapman, "Proposition 13: Causes and Impacts," paper prepared for the Conference on Tax Limitation, University of California, Santa Barbara, December 13–14, 1978; Jack Citrin, "Do People Want Something for Nothing: Public Opinion on Taxes and Spending," *National Tax Journal* 32:2 (June 1979), p. 116; and Advisory Commission on Intergovernmental Relations, *Changing Public Attitudes on Governments and Taxes, 1980* (Washington, D.C.: ACIR, 1980).

[1] Trust government always or most of the time (percentage agreeing)

[2] Government wastes of lot of tax money (percentage agreeing)

[3] Percentage voting in elections for U.S. House of Representatives

[4] Public officials don't care what people think (percentage agreeing)

[5] Property tax is the least fair tax (percentage agreeing)

[6] Goverment percentage of Gross National Product

[7] Consumer price index (percentage increase)

Figure 2–1. Measures Relevant to Electoral Politics

centage of gross national product consumed by government increased only very slightly over this time period, and even decreased before passage of the Jarvis-Gann Initiative. Inflation, measured as percentage change in the consumer price index, fluctuated in a generally upward trend over the period.

Finally, the perception that property taxes are the least fair tax changed little, but actually declined from its high point of the early 1970s before Proposition 13 reached the ballot, suggesting that fiscal limits, most of which are focused on this tax, arrived even as concern with them declined somewhat. One reason for this decline is the impact of inflation, pushing federal income-tax payers into higher brackets. In 1972, 19 percent of the respondents to the annual ACIR survey of attitudes toward government and taxes rated income tax "least fair" (compared to 45 percent so labeling local property taxes). By 1978, the two taxes were nearly even in this unpopularity poll (30 percent for the income tax versus 32 percent for the property tax). Indeed, this trend continued, and by 1980 36 percent of the respondents to this poll judged the income tax to be least fair while 25 percent so judged the property tax, a reversal made understandable by the continuation of inflation's impact on the federal income tax and the impact of the Fiscal Limits Movement in curbing the rise in property taxes (ACIR 1980, pp. 21–22).

Michael Boskin (1979) suggests that support for fiscal limits is a reaction to the total tax burden, not to specific taxes. He argues that by 1978, workers had experienced a half-decade in which real economic growth had declined precipitously from historical levels, that most of the growth that did occur flowed into government spending and not into personal disposable income, and that future prospects were for continued growth in tax levels as a result of already legislated increases and the elasticity of the whole tax structure. But what explains the emergence of a Fiscal Limits Movement that constrains the taxing and spending of state and local governments rather than that of the federal government, the source of the offending policies in Boskin's analysis?

John Shannon, Assistant Director of the ACIR, offers an analysis of the source of support for fiscal limits also rooted in economic factors (1981). He argues that total state and local expenditures as a percentage of the Gross National Product (GNP) increased from 9.6 percent in 1959 to 15.2 percent in 1975, and that a reaction by policymakers at all three levels beginning in 1976 sought to reverse this trend. In this analysis, formal fiscal limits are but one of the instruments employed to achieve a rebalancing of the proportion of the GNP going to state and local governments. While states increased taxes (586 tax increases and 46 new tax enactments) in the 1959–1976 period, 36 states reduced personal-income taxes, 9 indexed personal-income taxes, and 22 cut general sales-tax rates in the 1977–1980 period, the period encompassing fiscal limits. At the same time, federal grants-in-aid declined in constant dollars after 1978 and further sharp reductions were sought in the first Reagan budget.

To complete the analysis, the political factors confronting citizens must be included. In some states, direct electoral action spurred fiscal constraint;

in others, the policies of constraint developed by executives and legislators were consonant with public expectations. Citizens faced not only declining economic prospects but also an unwieldly and often recalcitrant political system. Parties, the traditional mechanism for linkage between citizens and elected officials, were weak. Citizens' identification with parties had declined, parties did not provide the resources candidates needed for election campaigns, nor were parties often effective mechanisms for leading and disciplining legislators (Ladd 1978). Ladd credits much of the impoverished state of parties to the impact of reformers whose zeal to open up party structures to wider participation ultimately made parties less able to perform traditional mobilization, brokerage, and leadership roles.

But even without the efforts of reformers, party structures would probably have declined in importance during the 1960s and 1970s. Parties are most relevant to jurisdictional elections and to jurisdictional policymaking. But the importance of jurisdictional elections and policymaking declined during this period. As more important policies were elaborated in the functionally specific systems that cut across jurisdictions, jurisdictional elections and policymaking declined somewhat in importance. Policies were influenced more by technicians who understood the linkages among jurisdictions of particular policies and programs.

Probably at least as important as any relative decline in the overall importance of jurisdictional politics was the changed opportunity structure that development of functional interest-based politics provided to state and federal legislators. No longer need they rely on the party or individuals and organizations within their districts for campaign finances and issue identification. Instead, they could become identified (usually through the legislation they advocated) with the position of one or another interest group, directly soliciting funds from those sympathetic to a position whether or not they reside in the legislator's district or are of similar political-party identification. The extremes to which this process may be taken were illustrated in a southern California congressional-election race in 1980 in which the Republican incumbent (Dornan) and Democratic challenger (Peck) each spent more than $2 million, but raised only about 10 percent of their campaign funds within the congressional district they were contesting. This style of "representation" and of raising resources for campaigns spurs members of legislative bodies to initiate policies that create supportive interest groups, as suggested earlier in the discussion of the increase in policy initiative by members of Congress.

Confronted by declining economic fortunes and an unwieldly political system better structured to increase benefits to specific constituencies than to cope with a general issue such as tax relief, citizens were essentially excluded from policy processes except as members of interest groups, and the electorate turned increasingly to fiscal limits as mechanisms that met several of their needs. Most obviously, fiscal limits provided taxpayers with an opportunity to alleviate their economic strain by reducing taxes. In California, for example, the total per capita state and local tax burden was reduced from $1,226 in FY 1977–1978 to $1,055 in FY 1978–1979, and the corresponding reduction in total state and local taxes per $1,000 of personal income was from $156 to $120 (Jamison 1980). In addition, the provisions of Proposition 13 that limit future increases in property taxes (no more than 2 percent annually except where ownership changes) introduced a certainty and a limit on the impact that increases in property tax could have on the personal budgets of California homeowners. This change is of tremendous economic value to those benefiting from it. Since property taxes had been increasing so dramatically in the three years prior to passage of the Jarvis-Gann Initiative, this tax, which is a tax on unreceived income, threatened the ability of many to retain ownership of their residences because their incomes were increasing much more slowly than were their property taxes. Moreover, the stipulation that any new special taxes require a two-thirds vote promised general constraint on increased taxation, a goal Californians pursued further by adopting Proposition 4 in November, 1979. The specifics of the California case are further analyzed in subsequent chapters, but the attraction of fiscal limits as an instrument to achieve relief from economic pressures is apparent.

On a political level, Proposition 13 and many other fiscal limits offer two related attractions to an electorate disaffected with prevailing political practices. First, in sharp contrast to the common perception that voting for candidates is often ineffective (the lament that the choice is often between Tweedle-dum and Tweedle-dee), voting for fiscal limits is a politically powerful exercise of choice. Where the fiscal-limits measure was placed on the ballot, the electorate had a choice to determine a specific policy of great importance. Voting for a candidate is always an imperfect expression of electoral preference because any member of the electorate has multiple preferences and any candidate represents multiple policy implications, so that perfect matches are virtually unobtainable. In addition, new issues arise between elections, issues on which the electorate may not even have a preference at the time of the election, with the result that the policy consequences of choosing among the limited number of candidates available in any election are unknown. Fiscal limits, in contrast, offered simpler, more direct linkage between choice and consequence. When a specific reduction in taxes was offered, the effects on personal budgets were easily calculable. When an institutional change was offered (such as a limit on expenditures), the calculations were less certain but still more certain in that regard than were choices among candidates. What *was* uncertain in voting for any fiscal limit was its potential impact on services. In both the case of Proposition 13 in California and Proposition 2½ in Massachusetts, citizens generally believed taxes could be cut substantially without reducing services (Citrin 1979; McDaniel 1981). The available evidence for these states suggests that services *are* affected by these two measures (the California case is examined later), implying that citizens miscalculated in this regard. However, in the California case, there is no evidence that if voters were again presented with an opportunity to vote on Proposition 13, the outcome would be any different.

The second political attraction of a vote on fiscal limits is that it entails direct citizen involvement in the political system. In terms of the analysis advanced here, it reasserts the importance of jurisdictional politics as the locus of all fiscal limits, and those voting for fiscal limits plausibly expect to at least create the fiscal boundaries of a political system, the policies of which they find it difficult to affect. This rationale helps to explain why citizens who are generally satisfied with governmental services will often vote for fiscal limits. In California, for example, a majority of survey respondents who wanted increased spending in up to four service areas voted for Proposition 13 (Citrin 1979 p. 122). Attitude surveys in Massachusetts reveal that nearly two-thirds of the respondents believed that California's experience with Proposition 13 had demonstrated that taxes could be cut without requiring service cuts, and that 82 percent of those holding this belief voted for Proposition 2½ (McDaniel, 1981 p. 5). Part of the explanation for these attitudes is found in beliefs that the elimination of graft, corruption, and inefficiencies would allow services to be provided with fewer dollars (beliefs apparently stronger in Massachusetts than in California), and part can be found in preferences for a shift in the mix of services (commonly more emphasis on police and fire departments and less on welfare and public-assistance services). But an election-day CBS survey on voters' reasons for voting for Proposition 13, that included as a possible response "It's a way to show what people want," found that 40 percent of those who voted for Proposition 13 chose this response, compared with 57 percent who chose property-tax cuts and 22 percent who contended that "Government provides many unnecessary services" (up to two responses were allowed) (CBS 1978, p. 2). Such sentiments are congruent with the general trend of declining approval of government.

Although cutting taxes, increasing governmental efficiency, or eliminating undesired services undoubtedly were the objectives of many voters who supported fiscal limits, a more general desire by citizens to affect the political system is also a plausible explanation of their vote. In California, citizens voting for fiscal limits did so despite predictions by virtually all government and business leaders that Proposition 13 would prove to be an unworkable disaster. This rejection of elite exhortation is among the more notable dimensions of Proposition 13 (and has also occurred in other states), providing strong evidence that the electorate did not trust those whose positions of power gave them greater participation in policy processes. In testimony before the Senate Subcommittee on Intergovernmental Relations in April, 1978, before the vote on Proposition 13, pollster Louis Harris argued that Americans rejected interest-group politics (for example, 71 percent agreed that "The trouble with getting something special for your group is that you'll end up paying for it four or five times over in higher taxes"). They also distrusted big government, big business, and big labor, and were desirous of both taking more responsibility for their own affairs and of effective governmental action on issues such as inflation which individuals could not affect (Harris 1978). The malaise concerning our political system is deep and widespread; fiscal limits may not cure the discomfort, but their attractiveness is at least partially based in these general evaluations of the condition of the body politic.

The appeal of fiscal limits has been powerful. Though measures are defeated on occasion, thirty-one states had at least one of the four contemporary types of fiscal limits by the end of 1979. Nearly all of these limits were adopted in the 1970s. Thirty states enacted limits in that decade. To illustrate the rapidity and strength of this movement, only sixteen states adopted the individual income tax, fifteen the corporate income tax, and twenty-four the general sales tax in the 1930s, the decade of most-frequent adoption of these three pillars of state and local revenue generation (ACIR 1980).

Table 2–3 provides a listing of the states that have adopted each of the four types of fiscal limits. *Full-disclosure laws* require automatic property-tax rate reductions to offset increased assessed valuation unless receipt of the increased revenue is justified in a rigorous full-disclosure procedure (such as public hearings). *Property-tax levy limits* constrain the total amount of property-tax revenues raised. *Expenditure lids,* as the label suggests, limit total expenditures. *Assessment constraints* involve some limit to keep property assessment increases below market-level increases (for example, Proposition 13 limits increases of assessed valuation of property that has not changed ownership to 2 percent annually, with the exception of utilities and oil properties that are reassessed annually).

Table 2–3
States with Contemporary Fiscal Limits

State	Full-Disclosure Laws	Property-Tax Levy Limits	Expenditure Lids	Assessment Constraints
Alaska		x		
Arizona	x	x	x	
California			x	x
Colorado		x		

Table 2-3 continued

State	Full-Disclosure Laws	Property-Tax Levy Limits	Expenditure Lids	Assessment Constraints
Delaware		x		
Florida	x	x		
Hawaii	x			
Idaho				x
Indiana		x		
Iowa		x	x	x
Kansas		x	x	
Kentucky	x	x		
Louisiana		x		
Maryland	x			x
Massachusetts		x	x	
Minnesota		x		x
Montana	x			
Nebraska			x	
Nevada			x	
New Jersey			x	
New Mexico		x		
Ohio		x		
Oregon		x		x
Rhode Island	x			
South Carolina		x		
Tennessee	x			
Texas	x			
Utah		x		
Virginia	x			
Washington		x		
Wisconsin		x		
Totals 31	10	19	8	6

Source: Adapted from the Advisory Commission on Intergovernmental Relations, *Significant Features of Fiscal Federation, 1979–1980* (Washington, D.C.: Advisory Commission on Intergovernmental Relations, 1980). Complete to November 1979.

Given the strength of the contextual factors related to the appeal of fiscal limits it is probable that still more states will enact such policies in the future. Forty states ultimately enacted property-tax rate limits, the approach to fiscal constraint of decades past. Rising property values reduced the effectiveness of this tax-control mechanism unless it was coupled with an assessment constraint, the Jarvis-Gann strategy. It is likely that forty states will enact modern fiscal limits before the end of this decade, although this is only a prognosis. Specific features of each state's public finance and political systems will, of course, influence the pace of further adoption of fiscal limits and the shape of whatever measures are enacted. The examination of the case of California's Proposition 13 presented in the next chapter shows the impact of the specific context of one state on the limits ultimately enacted.

3   Tax Reform in California

Passage of Proposition 13 in the June, 1978 California election was a cathartic event for both that state and the nation. Approval of this drastic fiscal limit by two-thirds of the voters in the nation's most populous and wealthy state broke the deadlock on tax reform in California and gave national prominence to a movement toward fiscal constraint that had already begun. This analysis of the California case illustrates the general phenomenon associated with movements toward fiscal limits already discussed and provides evidence of the specific contextual factors that have shaped them. The next two chapters also analyze the California case; chapter 4 analyzes the effects of fiscal limits on the fiscal system and on service delivery, and chapter 5 analyzes political impacts.

First the economic, political, and public-fiscal systems existing in California in the late 1970s will be examined. Attention then will be turned to the decade of efforts to reform California's tax system that preceded adoption of the Jarvis-Gann Initiative. Finally, the election campaigns for Proposition 13 and two related tax-limit measures (Proposition 4, approved in November, 1979, and Proposition 9, defeated in June, 1980) will be analyzed.

Context

Three elements of the California context are relevant to its experience with fiscal limits. The state is wealthy, with a strong economy and good prospects for future economic growth. Its political institutions are among the most reformed of any in the nation, incorporating virtually all of the elements proposed by several decades of reformers; and its legislature has been dominated by liberals for the past decade. Finally, patterns of revenues and expenditures of California state and local governments were also very distinctive prior to 1978, including high taxes, a very elastic (and largely progressive) tax system, and a pattern of expenditures congruent with a liberal, professionalized political system.

The Economy of California

California is wealthy. Were the state a nation, its Gross National Product would be the eighth largest in the world, just behind that of the United

Kingdom, and greater than that of Canada, Brazil, or Poland. The per-capita personal income of Californians exceeds the national average by more than 10 percent, although on this measure it is exceeded by Alaska, Nevada, and the District of Columbia. Moreover, the California economy is quite robust. In only one of the three most recent recessions has it fared worse than the national average, as measured by percentage declines in employment. In 1960–1962, when employment in the nation declined 2.1 percent, employment in California did not decline; in 1970–1971, when national employment declined 1.5 percent, employment in California declined 2.4 percent; in 1974–1975, national employment declined 3.2 percent, while the corresponding figure for California was 2.0 percent (ACIR 1980c, pp. 52–54). Unemployment rates in California are often higher than in the nation as a whole, but this is usually the consequence of job-seeking immigrants and of increasing labor-force participation rates. Job-creation rates are high in the state. Between 1970 and 1979, for example, the California population grew by 1.4 percent and the civilian labor force by 3.3 percent annually (Security Pacific National Bank 1980, p. 30). In contrast, the national civilian labor force expanded at the rate of 2.5 percent annually during this period. Security Pacific National Bank forecasts that the California labor force will expand at a 3.3 percent annual rate through 1985, while employment will grow at a 3.2-percent rate, both figures above the national rates (1980).

The impact of this wealth and strong economy on the politics of the state is pervasive. Some policy issues, such as the provision of new housing, protection of the environment, or procurement of water and energy, are pushed to the forefront of policymaking by this economic situation, while others such as job retraining, or the decay of cities, are less pressing than in other parts of the nation. Economic growth results in pressure for expanded government, especially to provide the capital infrastructure needed to accommodate increased population and employment. The economic wealth of the state has created the expectation, especially among government officials, that public services will be in ample supply and of high quality. The state's public sector was generally very well endowed in the years preceeding passage of Proposition 13, as will be seen in the section on revenue and expenditure patterns.

The Political System of California

California's political institutions are of the "reformed" variety and its public employees are highly professionalized. All California local governments hold nonpartisan elections. The council-manager form of government predominates in cities, and even the largest cities and counties have chief administrative officers who possess more stature and power than average. Public employment has historically been structured on the civil-service model, with competitive examinations for entry and promotion, and merit principles; more recently, collective bargaining has been mandated by the state legislature. The legislature is itself highly professionalized, with essentially full-time legislators and a large supporting staff. In 1971, the Citizens Conference on State Legislatures ranked the California legislature first in the nation on a weighted scale including five categories (functionality, accountability, informedness, independence, and representativeness)(Leach and O'Rourke 1975, pp. 183–184). Had a similar survey been conducted at the end of the 1970s, the California legislature would certainly have been very high in such a ranking and would probably have retained its lead position, although some observers contend that the professionalized legislature has not proven any more capable of solving California's problems than have less reformed legislative bodies (Margolis 1976).

Political parties are weak in California. Much of this weakness is the legacy of Progressives who instituted a number of reforms in California electoral law in the 1911 and 1913 legislative sessions in an attempt to break the domination of California politics by the Southern Pacific Railway. The Southern Pacific exercised control of the state legislature through the Republican Party, control of Los Angeles and San Francisco by political machines, and controlled most of the balance of the state by threats to withhold rail service. It was an overwhelming political force for three decades. With the election of Progressive Hiram Johnson to the governorship in 1910 and the election of a number of like-minded legislators, cross-filing (by which candidates could file in both Republican and Democratic primaries, a procedure abolished in 1959) the referendum, initiative, and recall were adopted (Owens, Costantini, and Weschler 1970, pp. 33–36). The direct primary was subsequently adopted, removing parties from any formal role in selecting candidates for office.

The consequences of these political-structure factors are powerful. Professionalized public services became bureaucracies, now the norm in California state and local government, and embraced certain values. The most powerful of these values include an emphasis on service provision as the central role of government, a tendency to equate uniformity of treatment of cases with equity, and the frequent use of at least the tools of rationality (such as productivity studies and benefit-cost analysis) in decision making. These three values are widely influential because they are reinforced by both the norms of individual professional behavior and the strictures of bureaucratic forms of organization. Professionals are expected to provide services equitably according to rational judgments. Bureaucracies provide services as outputs, their standard operating procedures encourage equal treatment of like cases, and norms of rationality mold their decision making.

Of course, these three values are never perfectly realized, but they are powerful influences upon the behavior of state and local officials in California. Even if only invoked as "motive talk," (the socially legitimizing language explaining behavior), they shape action (Cochran 1980). In California, the values are also institutionalized in organizations and individual roles. City managers are expected to be professional managers and contributors of rationality to policy processes. The state legislature receives professional analytic advice from five distinct organizations designed solely for this purpose (Legislative Analyst's Office, Senate Office of Research, Assembly Office of Research, Legislative Counsel, and Auditor General); each committee of the legislature also has an analytic staff to support its activities. Most California state bureaucracies and many local governments maintain organization subunits for analysis and evaluation. In the discussion of the shape of the California public sector and the history of tax reform that follows, the impact of these values will become evident.

The California legislature requires further analysis, both because of its centrality to events preceding and following passage of Proposition 13, and because its dynamics diverge significantly from the three values just discussed. Some description of the legislature has already been provided: it is a full-time body with extensive staff support existing in a state political system characterized by weak political parties. To understand the behavioral consequences of these features, consider the opportunity and incentive structures confronted by an aspirant to the legislature or by legislators. Bereft of the traditional functions of political parties (selection of candidates, management of campaigns, provision of campaign financing, identification to voters), legislators essentially stand alone before the electorate. Each individual aspirant must strive for personal visibility because the party plays little role in candidate selection. Although two-thirds of the legislative seats are relatively safe for incumbents of one party or the other (Fair Political Practices Commission (FPPC) 1980, p. 35), California legislators must continue to strive for individual visibility to raise campaign contributions.

Campaigns for the California Assembly and Senate are expensive. In 1978, the year of the Jarvis-Gann Initiative, for example, median and high expenditures for the primary and general elections are shown in table 3–1. The FPPC reports that major-party candidates for competitive Senate seats (for which the winner received from 50 to 60 percent of the two-party vote) in the 1978 general election spent a median amount of $214,763. Assembly candidates in like circumstance spent $100,520. Of contributions available for spending in the 1980 election, the average amount received from large interest groups (over $1,000, excluding political parties and individuals except other legislators) was $248,600 for those winning election to the Senate and $189,775 for those winning election to the Assembly (Salzman,

Table 3–1
Campaign Expenditures of California Senate and Assembly
Candidates, 1978
(dollars)

Legislative Body	Median	High	Number of Candidates Reporting
Senate			
Primary	12,772	181,784	67
General	51,605	346,226	39
Assembly			
Primary	14,653	164,047	274
General	42,861	301,404	153

Source: State of California, Fair Political Practices Commission, *Campaign Costs: How Much Have They Increased and Why?* (Sacramento: FPPC, 1980).

1981a). Campaign costs are increasing. In constant-dollar-per-vote cost, for example, Senate campaign costs increased from nine cents in 1958, to fifteen cents in 1968 and thirty-five cents in 1978. For the Assembly, the equivalent costs were ten cents, twenty-three cents, and forty-seven cents, (FPPC 1980, p. 27).

The currency that incumbent legislators have to play with in this game of electoral politics takes two forms: bills and committee assignments. The importance of both to interest groups is apparent: bills give advantage and disadvantage to interest groups and committees are the arenas of the most intense legislative activity concerning them. Given the opportunity and incentive structure they confront in obtaining campaign funds for reelection campaigns, legislators may be expected to use the introduction of bills and committee assignments to increase their capacities to generate campaign contributions. As a result, bill introductions may be expected to be numerous and competition for committee assignments with well-endowed clientele to be fierce. By and large, the behavior of California legislators bears out these expectations.

Bill introductions are nearly rampant. In 1978, for example, 3,839 bills were introduced in the Assembly and 2,250 in the Senate, an average of nearly fifty bills per member of the lower house and nearly sixty per member of the upper house. Moreover, a large volume of bills become law. In that year, 1,605 Assembly bills and 1,029 Senate bills ultimately became law; 2,639 bills ultimately became part of the statutes of California in 1978. By comparison, the average annual rate of bill introduction in all state legislatures in 1975–1976 was 1,975, with an annual average of 426 bills passed (Rosenthal and Forth 1978).

Competition for committee assignments is waged in contests for leadership of the Assembly and Senate. In 1979 and 1980, for example, the California legislature was wracked by three leadership struggles. Carol Hallet unseated Paul Priolo as leader of the Republicans (the minority party) in the Assembly in May, 1979. David Roberti unseated James Mills as the head of the Senate Democrats in early 1980. But the largest fight of all, in late 1979 and most of 1980, was the challenge of Howard Berman to Leo McCarthy for the Office of Speaker of the Assembly, widely considered to be the second-most-powerful position in California state government. Berman charged that McCarthy was paying too much attention to his aspirations for statewide office and not enough to the needs of fellow Assembly Democrats. Both sides sought to elect more supporters in the November election; McCarthy raised $1,188,000 and Berman $763,000 in 1979 and 1980, most of which was spent in support of Democratic candidates favorable to their campaigns for the Office of Speaker. Berman and McCarthy each succeeded in unseating an incumbent Democratic assemblyman supportive of the other. Partly because of Democratic members' reaction to this internecine warfare and partly because of an alliance with Assembly Republicans, Willie Brown, the flamboyant Black assemblyman from San Francisco, was ultimately elected Speaker in late November, 1980 (Pollard 1981).

Members of the California legislature successful in achieving election and reelection exhibit attributes reflective of the political system in which they operate. In turn, these attributes affect their behavior; the deliberations of the legislature on tax reform in the decade before adoption of Proposition 13, to be examined shortly, provide evidence of such impacts. As shown in table 3-2, among the most important attributes of the 1977–1978 legislature was the frequency of *political* careers among members: 48 percent of all legislators and 62 percent of the members of the Assembly had always been politicians, and many began political careers in college and thereafter pursued such careers as their dominant interests. A quarter of the membership of the Assembly worked as political staff members prior to running for office. Only a third had served as local-government elected officials before election to the legislature. Such career paths encourage the emergence of legislators who define politics as the accommodation and manipulation of interest groups, and provide tutelage in the strategies for generating campaign contributions and campaigning for office. Because their life experiences are so heavily political, personal knowledge of business, farming, or the arts is almost unusual. Moreover, the political arena of most familiarity is the state legislature; these members are not widely experienced in local government.

Perhaps partly because of this career pattern, and at least partly a reflection of the attitudes of the electorate, the California legislature was usually liberal on social and fiscal issues during the later 1970s. The legis-

Table 3–2
Attributes of Members of the California Legislature, 1977–1978 Session
(percentages)

	Assembly	Senate	Total
Percentage of members with substantially political careers[a]	62	22	48
Percentage of members who had served as staff to elected officials prior to their election	24	2	17
Percentage of members who identify self as "full-time" legislators	32	22	29
Percentage of members who had held local-government elective office	38	20	32

Source: Calculated from biographical data provided in State of California, *California Legislature, 1977* (Sacramento: State of California, 1977).

[a]Defined as those first elected to the legislature before the age of forty, or who did not have at least ten years of nonpolitical employment, counting years as staff to elected officials as political employment.

lative leadership in the years immediately preceding passage of Proposition 13 was undeniably liberal, seeking opportunities to use their powers for redistributive purposes and generally desirous of an expanded public sector. In the specific case of tax reform, for example, a case to be further analyzed, *every* proposal that received leadership support in the two legislative sessions preceding passage of the Jarvis-Gann Initiative sought at least to maintain the existing state revenues and to direct any tax relief to those of lower economic station.

The Public Sector of California

Before the Jarvis-Gann Initiative, the California public sector was supported by high levels of taxation, an elastic revenue-generation system, and expenditure patterns consonant with those expected of a political system in which political parties are weak.

In FY 1977–1978, California ranked third highest among all states (behind Alaska and New York) in total state and local tax collections per capita ($1,226) and fourth in tax collections per $1,000 of personal income ($156)(Jamison 1980). California was above the national norm in receipts from the most powerful taxes: on a per-capita basis, it ranked fifth among all states in property taxes, twelfth in sales taxes, thirteenth in personal-income taxes, second in taxes in corporation net income, and third in gift and death taxes (Jamison 1980).

Moreover, the California tax system was elastic, capturing increasing shares as growth and inflation increased personal income and property values. In the four years from FY 1973-1974 to FY 1977-1978, total state and local tax revenues increased by 71.7 percent, while personal income increased by only 55.5 percent. During this period, the burden of taxation increased more rapidly in California than elsewhere in the nation. For example, in FY 1973-1974, California tax collections per $1,000 of personal income were 115 percent of the equivalent figure for the balance of the nation ($141.48 versus $123.02); by FY 1977-1978, they were 126.7 percent of that figure ($156.23 versus $123.31)(Jamison 1980). Table 3-3 shows the elasticities of selected California taxes for the FY 1973-1974 to FY 1977-1978 period. Property-tax revenues grew nearly as rapidly as did personal income, while the other taxes all outstripped growth in personal income; the personal-income tax being prodigiously productive of increased tax revenue to the state government.

While collected taxes soared, especially at the state level, in the years preceding passage of the Jarvis-Gann Inititive, expenditures did not accelerate so rapidly. Jamison compared general-expenditure and tax-revenue patterns in California to a national norm, computed as the expenditures and revenues that would have occurred had the national average rates of taxation and expenditure per $1,000 of personal income been applied in California. Table 3-4 reports these data, showing that total expenditures by California governments did not greatly exceed the national norms. Some previously high-expenditure items moved toward the national norm in the decade preceding Jarvis-Gann. Expenditures for welfare declined from 93.1 percent above the national average in FY 1966-1967 to 44.2 percent greater in FY 1977-1978. Education declined from 13.6 percent to 8.7 percent greater than the national norm. But much of the explanation for the low total expenditures was found in abnormally low capital outlays by California governments. Jamison calculated that California state and local government underexpended from 25 to 30 percent on capital outlays compared with the national average per $1,000 of personal income, a sum of $1 to 1.4 billion annually. Most of the capital outlay shortfall occurred in outlays for highways, for which California spent less per $1,000 of personal income in FY 1977-1978 than did all but two other states. This discrepancy between revenues and expenditures resulted in the accumulation of surplus funds, especially at the state level. At the time of the passage of Proposition 13, the accumulated state general fund surplus was $3.4 billion, of which nearly half had resulted from underestimates of personal-income-tax receipts.

The number of California state and local employees per 1,000 popula-

Table 3-3
Expansion of Selected California Taxes Relative to Growth in
Personal Income, 1973-1978

Tax	Ratio to Personal Income
Total state and local taxes	1.10
Property tax	.99
Individual income tax	1.65
Corporate income tax	1.28
General sales tax	1.15

Source: Calculated from Conrad Jamison, *California Tax Study* (Los Angeles: Security Pacific National Bank, 1980).

Table 3-4
California State and Local Taxes and General Expenditures
Compared with National Norms
(percentages)

Fiscal Year	Tax Revenues	General Expenditures
1973-1974	+ 15.0	+ 10.5
1974-1975	+ 21.7	+ 7.1
1975-1976	+ 21.3	+ 8.7
1976-1977	+ 22.8	+ 5.9
1977-1978	+ 26.7	+ 9.8

Source: Conrad Jamison, *California Tax Study* (Los Angeles: Security Pacific National Bank, 1980).

tion has increased consistently since World War II and was 13.7 percent above the national average for this ratio in 1977. Employment in public education was especially strong, increasing from 9.9 employees per 1,000 population in 1946 to 27.2 in 1968 (15.7 percent above the national average) and 35.7 in 1977 (21.4 percent above the national average). In the mid-1970s, this growth occurred while school enrollments declined. Employment in California state and local government other than in education grew less precipitously: from 16.3 employees per 1,000 population in 1946 to 24.2 in 1968 (9.5 percent above the national average) to 29.2 in 1977 (5.4 percent above the national average) (calculated from Jamison 1979).

The impression of California state and local government emerging from these data shows a well-endowed public sector, with an expansive revenue base and more control over expenditures than over revenues raised. This pattern is consonant with the biases expected of reformed, professionalized political systems, which typically have higher taxation and general-fund expenditures, but lower debt and capital expenditures than do old-style party and machine political systems (Erie 1980). Moreover, the liberal cast of California politics is seen in the patterns of its revenue generation and expenditures. In regard to taxes, the growth in personal-income taxes was considered desirable by liberal legislators because that tax is progressive, including features that make it even more progressive than the federal income tax in some regards (no dividend exclusion, less favorable treatment of capital gains, and steeply progressive rates through middle-range incomes). Personal-income taxes supported 26 percent of state general-fund expenditures in FY 1970–1971; by FY 1978–1979, that proportion had risen to 39 percent. Even the increase in property-tax collections from owners of single-family residences (from 34.8 percent of all property taxes collected in FY 1970–1971 to 42.2 percent in FY 1977–1978) was viewed as desirable by those who saw it as a mechanism to tax wealth, a sentiment that dominated legislators' consideration of tax reform in the 1976–1978 period. In regard to expenditures, even though California became more like other states in the 1970s, it spent 38 percent ($1.4 billion) more on welfare than the average amount per $1,000 of per-capita income in other states in FY 1976–1977, 6 percent ($672 million) more on education, and 54 percent ($221 million) more on local parks and recreation (Jamison 1979), all testimony to a liberal orientation in public policymaking.

Even within these expenditure patterns, there is some evidence that the professionalized, reformed governments of California deemphasized direct-service provision in the years preceding Proposition 13, placing increasing percentages of public employees in staff, supervisory, and ancillary positions. In an insightful and thorough study of the city of Los Angeles from FY 1972–1973 through FY 1977–1978, Chaiken and Walker (1979) found that while expenditures rose by 64 percent (more than 10 percent annually), direct services received by citizens almost certainly declined. Although inflation consumed nearly 60 percent of the increased funds available, (including pay increases generally consistent with increases in price indices and compensation in the private sector), the next largest contributor (11.1 percent) to increased costs was a shift in employee mix toward higher-paid job categories not involved in direct-service provision. The shift involved not only an increase in the number of personnel in overhead as opposed to direct-service departments, but also a movement within departments away from service provision to administrative and support roles (Chaiken and Walker 1979, p. 50–52). On-the-street police and fire personnel declined in this period, for example. This elaboration of higher-level roles is consistent with the professional ethic, and was quite probably also encouraged by the increasing complexity and interdependence of the intergovernmental system during this time (as discussed in chapter 2).

Prelude

Tax reform was a prominent issue in California politics in the decade before passage of Proposition 13. If more substantial reform had occurred between 1968 and 1978, the Jarvis-Gann Initiative would probably not have been adopted. Three periods of tax reform can be identified. In each period tax reform from the state legislature was usually forthcoming only under strong outside pressure; pressure that was usually applied via initiatives that proposed reforms to which the legislature then developed counterproposals. A second constant throughout the three periods of tax reform was the image of desirable tax reform that dominated legislative policymaking. Any tax reform should be *balanced,* that is, provide new revenues to replace any yielded by reform, and be redistributive, helping most the economically disadvantaged.

Modest Tax Reforms Repel Radical Initiatives, 1968–1975

In the first period, 1968–1975, the legislature achieved a series of modest tax reforms, and two radical referenda were defeated. The legislative enactments directed tax relief to certain classes of taxpayers and were balanced in order to generate additional revenues to offset any lost through the aid targeted to specific groups. The period was initiated in 1968 by three property-tax exemptions: a $750 homeowners exemption, total exemption of household personal property, and a 15 percent exemption of business inventory. Senate Bill (SB) 90, passed on the last day of the 1972 legislative session in a successful effort to defuse a more radical initiative launched by Los Angeles County Assessor Philip Watson, was the most significant tax reform prior to Proposition 13 and exemplifies the tax-reform politics of this period. The homeowner's exemption was raised from $750 to $1,750 of assessed value; a sliding income-tax exemption was increased from 15 to 50 percent; and the state increased subventions for education. The $1 billion in costs was financed by increased sales, bank and corporation taxes, and by drawing upon surplus state revenues and the just-arriving federal revenue-sharing funds. A tax-rate limit was placed on cities, counties, and special districts (the limit proved ineffective when assessed valuations increased). School districts were placed under an expenditure limitation that effectively limited revenue increases by tying them to enrollments and inflation. Votes of the electorate were required to override these limits. In addition, the state was (with only limited success) prohibited from mandating activities to be performed by local governments without providing any funds needed for the accomplishment of such activities.

Two radical initiatives were defeated in this period. The main features of the Watson Initiative of 1972 (Proposition 13) were: to limit property taxes to a ceiling of 1.75 percent of market value, to remove welfare and community colleges from property-tax support, to limit the use of property taxes for schools (while mandating a uniform tax rate for schools), and to finance any resultant deficits by increased sales taxes and the imposition of special taxes upon liquor, cigarettes, and mining profits. In 1974, Governor Reagan sponsored Proposition 1, which froze property-tax rates at the maximum then in effect, tied total state appropriations to a percentage of the annual growth in aggregate personal income, prohibited state tax increases without voter approval, mandated the return of state surpluses to taxpayers, guaranteed state funding for state-mandated local programs, and reduced the state personal-income tax. Proposition 1 was narrowly defeated (2.3 million to 2 million votes).

Paralysis, 1975–1977

Despite the message embodied in the close defeat of the Reagan initiative and growing citizen unrest over increasing property taxes, the 1975–1977 period was one of paralysis. Many tax-reform bills were introduced; no major reforms passed, although modest extensions of relief to the elderly and to renters occurred in 1976. Most proposals sought to provide relief to homeowners through one of three main approaches—a split roll allowing homeowners to be taxed at a lower rate, a freeze on increased assessment, and increased homeowner relief. Though the relief sought was relatively modest, the mechanisms devised were often complex and the policy debates were arduous. The initiative process was also paralyzed at this time; several efforts failed to qualify for the ballot. But a factor that would make paralysis even more politically hazardous was emerging: unanticipated surpluses of current revenues in relation to current expenditures. As late as the summer of 1975, a deficit was projected for the FY 1975–1976 state budget, but by December a surplus of $463 million was anticipated, and a $641 million surplus was ultimately received. The FY 1976–1977 budget was signed in July, 1976, projecting a surplus in that year's accounts of nearly $800 million (later reduced to $230 million by subsequent appropriations). But the fiscal year closed with an estimated $2.7-billion addition to the state surplus, totaling $3.8 million. This generated increased pressure for tax relief and challenged the norm of balancing, of seeking new revenues to cover anticipated revenue losses.

Futile Complexity, 1977–1978

Governor Brown's State of the State message to the legislature in January, 1977 gave highest priority to property-tax reform. Many tax-reform bills were introduced in the 1977 session, but legislative deliberation focused on three (SB 12, Smith; SB 154, Petris; and Assembly Bill (AB) 999, Brown). These bills shared several features, especially their complexity, resulting in part from the aggregation of several extant proposals into each of the bills. All three bills also shared certain specific features: circuit breakers for both home owners and renters, split-roll assessments, and relief to local governments for the costs of state-mandated programs. They differed in the specific mechanisms by which these devices were to work, and in the incorporation of other features (for example, SB 154 and AB 999 widened the state income-tax brackets and raised the maximum rate from 11 to 15 percent).

The proposals advanced were complex, and one of their salutory effects was that they required improved information on the financing of the several thousand governments in the state and on the effects of alternative taxes on different categories of taxpayers and jurisdictions. A great improvement in the extent and quality of data relevant to these issues was achieved during 1977, accomplished largely through the interaction of the staff of the relevant legislative committees and state agencies in an ad hoc group called the Impacts Data Task Force. AB 999 (Brown), for example, included a circuit breaker for homeowners, renter relief, senior citizens' property-tax deferral, procedures for reimbursing local governments for state-mandated costs, assessment reform, a split property-assessment roll (to obtain lower rates of taxation on homeowners) and revenue limits on local and state governments. The revenue losses resulting from these various tax-relief proposals were to be offset by deletion of several tax-expenditure features of the existing sales and income taxes, and higher personal-income-tax rates. Calculating the impact of such complex legislation on taxpayers is a formidable task given the interactions among various taxes and differential impacts on taxpayers of different circumstance.

The continued liberal bias of the legislature was strongly evident in this period, both in the major tax-relief bills presented and in the analyses supporting them. AB 999, for example, was estimated by staff of the Assembly Revenue and Taxation Committee to reduce the taxes of an elderly, low-fixed-income single taxpayer by $314, to reduce the taxes of a family with average income and home value by $135, and to increase the taxes of an upper-income family with capital gains and a higher-value home by $38. A particularly important question for these policymakers was the incidence of the property tax on different income groups. It was well known that single-family residences were paying an increased share of the total property tax (35.5 percent in FY 1972–1973 compared with 41.4 percent in FY 1977–1978), the consequence of increased housing prices and a professionalized reassessment procedure that kept assessed values close to market prices. The strong liberal bias in the legislature was evident in their reaction to this shift. Rather than simply redressing the shift, they sought to maintain high property taxes on higher-value homes as a tax on wealth.

Table 3-5
California Home Values, Income, and Property Taxes, 1976

Adjusted Gross Income[a] (dollars)	Average Taxable Value[b] (dollars)	Average Property Taxes[c] (dollars)	Property Taxes as Percentage of Income
5,000	21,000	420	8.4
7,500	26,000	570	7.6
10,000	26,000	570	5.7
12,500	27,000	600	4.8
15,000	27,000	600	4.0
17,500	28,000	630	3.6
20,000	29,000	660	3.3
25,000	32,000	750	3.0
30,000	35,000	840	2.8
40,000	47,000	1,200	3.0
50,000	55,000	1,440	2.8
60,000	60,000	1,590	2.7
70,000	61,000	1,620	2.3
80,000	74,000	2,010	2.5
90,000	80,000	2,190	2.4
100,000	87,000	2,400	2.4

Source: Franchise Tax Board, as reported in State of California, Assembly Revenue and Taxation Committee, *Compilation of Statements and Partial Transcript* (Sacramento: State of California, 1976).

Note: There is a large variability between home values and income. Figures are based on 1975 returns for the 1974 income year; married couple, joint return.

[a]Excludes transfer payments such as Social Security, unemployment payments, Medi-Cal, and so on.

[b]Based on actual assessment data (3/1/1974 lien date).

[c]Based on $12.00 property-tax rate, including Homeowners' Exemption.

Of course, the property tax is not calculated on current income, so the ability of owners of expensive homes to pay the increased taxes is important to the feasibility of such plans. Table 3-5 presents the analysis of this question prepared for the legislature by its staff in late 1976. This analysis suggests that the property tax is not a high percentage of income; indeed, because the property tax appears here to be regressive, falling hardest on those with lower incomes, a case can be made that the tax should be increased on higher-valued homes so that the property tax is at least proportional to income.

This line of thought, bolstered by analyses such as that reproduced in table 3-5, dominated the California legislature's deliberations on tax reform in the months immediately preceding adoption of the Jarvis-Gann Initiative. But the conclusions concerning the relationship between housing values (and hence property taxes) and income suggested by this table were grossly inaccurate from 1976 onward. Although the median housing price in

California was close to the national norm in 1974 (in the $30,000 range), housing prices accelerated rapidly in California beginning in 1975, and by mid-1978 when voters entered the polling booths to vote on Proposition 13, the median housing price was over $80,000, 50 percent above the national median price. Median family incomes increased at about 10 percent annually during this period, a rate less than half as rapid as the increase in home prices. The analysis in table 3-5 was misleading because it reported housing values established in assessments in the 1971-1974 period (reassessment occurred at the time of purchase or in two- or three-year cycles), before the sharp jump in housing prices. The most interesting questions concerning table 3-5 are how it could have been proffered as serious analysis and how the perceptions it encouraged concerning the relationship between home values and income could have persisted so strongly. Part of the explanation can be found in the fact that the prices of housing in Sacramento, (housing most visible to the legislative staff and to many of the legislators), did not accelerate as rapidly as did housing prices in the area within fifty miles of the Pacific Ocean, the strip that contains most of the state's population. But the more fundamental explanation lies in the insularity of the California legislature, and in the persistence of the idea that tax reform *should* be redistributive and that the public sector *should* expand. This is powerful evidence of the importance of the political and ideational sectors of the political-process model advanced in the first chapter. New ideas/realities were effectively screened out because no political structures existed to bring them into the legislative arena, giving virtually free rein to the legislature to construct a definition of the "problem" of tax relief and of possible responses that were congruent with its values. The liberal biases of the legislators and their staff were so dominant as to exclude discordant information and prohibit development of tax-reform measures that did not provide for continued growth of state revenues and a redistributive tilt to any tax relief granted.

Catharsis

Proposition 13 qualified for the ballot on December 23, 1977, with 1,264,000 signatures, over twice the number required. The initiative process used to put the Jarvis-Gann property-tax-relief measure before the electorate is, as discussed earlier, a legacy of the reforms of the Progressive era adopted by the California electorate in 1911. Through 1979, 434 initiative petitions were circulated, 165 qualified for the ballot, and only 45 of these were approved (State of California, Secretary of State 1979). In comparison with the thousands of bills introduced and statutes enacted annually by the California legislature, the launching of an initiative is a rare event, and the adoption of such a nonlegislative enactment rarer still, occurring on the average less than once annually. Of course, the initiative has always been intended to be, and should remain, the exceptional rather than the normal form of policymaking, to be invoked when normal legislative processes fail.

Proposition 13 is a prototypical example of the use of the initiative process to break a legislative deadlock. Tax reform had been a pressing political issue in the state for at least a decade. Some tax relief had been provided, often in response to the threat of a more radical initiative proposal. But the legislators' definition of "the tax problem" and of conceivable responses ultimately proved unacceptable to the electorate. Indeed, the legislature itself was close to a deadlock on this issue, approving none of the tax-reform proposals considered during the 1977 legislative session, despite the increasing clamor for tax reform and the burgeoning state surplus.

The weight of complexity and the impossibility of pleasing all interests led to defeat. Under the threat of the impending vote on the Jarvis-Gann Initiative, the Behr bill (SB 1) was passed and signed by the governor in March, 1978. The bill, which would take effect only if its enabling constitutional amendment (Proposition 8) passed and Proposition 13 failed, provided for a split role, limited increases in property tax to the GNP deflator for state and local services, provided further property-tax relief by state assumption of major county health and welfare costs, expanded senior citizens', renters', and welfare recipients' relief, and set aside future state revenues in excess of a personal-income growth index for additional taxpayer relief. The cost of the program was estimated to be $1.4 billion in its first year.

Proposition 13 contrasted sharply with the complexity that characterized legislative tax-reform proposals of the previous decade, and with Proposition 8, the legislature's last bid to forestall ceding policymaking to the initiative process. Proposition 13 did not fit within the parameters that had shaped prior legislative deliberations. Instead it shattered those assumptions and created a new set of ground rules. Jarvis-Gann provided $7 billion in property-tax relief, a sum much larger than that proposed by the legislature; contained no provision for varying relief among classes of property-tax payers; made no provision for replacement revenues; and cut deeply at local governments' ability to raise revenues (reducing property-tax collections by 60 percent, equivalent to a 22 percent reduction in total expenditures). It dramatically altered intergovernmental relationships in California (reducing local governments' ability to raise own-source revenues, thus making them more dependent on state and federal transfers), and contained no provision for relieving local governments of any existing expenditure obligations nor any guarantees against future unfunded state mandates.

Voter approval of Proposition 13, of course, should not be interpreted as approval of all of these consequences. Instead, that overwhelming approval is better understood as the consequence of three attributes of the proposition. First, it cut property taxes, the source of major concern to California voters. Second, it provided opportunity to vent hostility against distrusted politicians, who had been unable to provide property-tax relief. Third, it provided certainty in a turbulent world in which citizens could find no other means to act generally against inflation and specifically against increased property taxes. Under Proposition 13, future property-tax payments became predictable: unless the property owner moved, increases would not exceed 2 percent annually; if a new residence was purchased, the new-property tax was 1 percent of the purchase price, and would thereafter increase by no more than 2 percent annually.

The full text of Proposition 13 is presented in appendix 3A. The brevity and simplicity of the proposed tax-relief measure is apparent. Voters were offered a tax-relief proposal far simpler and easier to comprehend than any of the measures considered by the legislature in the previous decade and also simpler than the three tax-reform initiatives previously rejected. Despite its apparent simplicity, Proposition 13 used language that created some uncertainty as to how it was to be implemented. For example, there was no "state law" to apportion remaining property-tax revenues (Section 1.a); no mention of what was to happen to the existing homeowners exemption; and no legal definition of "qualified electors" (Section 4), among other ambiguities.

While those campaigning against Proposition 13 sought to convince the electorate that these inadequacies in language were serious deficiencies and that there would be too much tax relief going to the wrong taxpayers (much was said about the fact that only one-third of the property-tax relief would go to homeowners), those advocating the initiative primarily emphasized that it would provide property-tax relief that had not been forthcoming from legislative political processes.

Expenditures in the election campaign for and against Proposition 13 were about equal ($2,152,874 and $2,000,204, respectively). But the sources of the contributions were very different. Only $166,853 of the contributions in support of Proposition 13 were $1,000 or greater, while $1,205,770 of the opposing contributions were of that magnitude. Opponents of Proposition 13 included not only most elected public officials, the overwhelming majority of professional public administrators, and many public-employee unions, but also the largest corporations and financial institutions, the League of Women Voters, and the California Taxpayers Association—a formidable array.

Table 3-6 reports the evidence from attitude polls conducted in the months preceding the June, 1978 ballot on the Jarvis-Gann Initiative. Only slightly more than half of the respondents knew of the measure in February, 1978, and less than a third of the respondents had an opinion, but support-

Table 3-6
Polled Attitudes toward Proposition 13
(percentages)

Poll Date	Responses before Explanation of Proposition 13 and Proposition 8				Responses after Explanation of Proposition 13 and Proposition 8		
	Know Of	*Support*	*Oppose*	*Undecided*	*Support*	*Oppose*	*Undecided*
February, 1978	56	20	10	20	—	—	—
March/April, 1978	70	27	25	18	—	—	—
Late April, 1978	—	41	34	25	37	46	17
Late May, 1978	—	52	35	13	48	40	12

Source: Reports on Field poll and *Times* poll, *Los Angeles Times,* April 12, May 7, May 28, 1978.

ers outnumbered opposers two to one. By late March/early April, after the legislature and the governor had elaborated their counterproposal in the form of SB 1 (Behr, R) and its enabling constitutional amendment, Proposition 8 (also to appear on the June, 1978 ballot), 70 percent of the respondents knew of the initiative, and about a quarter had positive and a quarter negative evaluations of the measure. In the next poll reported, conducted in late April, the number of supporters outnumbered those in opposition, until the features of both Proposition 13 and Proposition 8 were explained to the survey respondent, after which 46 percent opposed Proposition 13, 37 percent supported it, and 17 percent were undecided. This poll heartened the opponents of Proposition 13, whose campaign was based on the premise that if voters knew that less than the majority of the tax reductions resulting would go to homeowners and that public services would be cut, they would vote against Proposition 13 and for Proposition 8. But these hopes were dashed in the late-May poll that showed that explanation of the features of the opposing ballot measures only slightly reduced the percentage of respondents supporting Proposition 13 (from 52 percent to 48 percent). An intervening event usually credited with solidifying support for Proposition 13 was the release of property reassessments by Los Angeles County Assessor Alexander Pope in mid-May, reassessments ranging to over 100 percent on existing assessed values of residences. Widely reported in the news media, this sharp reassessment served to focus voter attention on the substantial property-tax reduction that was available in Proposition 13.

Sixty-five percent of those voting on June 6, 1978 voted for Proposition 13. Only once before had the initiative process successfully been used to reduce a tax: in 1914, the poll tax had been abolished by initiative. Seventy-six other initiatives dealing with taxation had either failed to qualify or had been rejected at the ballot box. Support for Proposition 13 came from most traditional analytic categories of voters. A majority of Blacks (51 percent), liberals (57 percent), renters (51 percent), and members of families of public employees (53 percent) opposed the measure, but by small proportions (CBS, 1978). Predictably, Republicans (73 percent) were more likely to support Jarvis-Gann than Democrats (53 percent), and 75 percent of the self-reported conservatives also supported Proposition 13. Seventy percent of those voting for Jarvis-Gann believed its passage would not affect local service levels, but 78 percent of those opposing it believed it would. If service cuts were necessary, cuts in welfare were preferred by both supporters (69 percent) and opponents (43 percent) of Proposition 13. On the basis of extensive analysis of available surveys of attitudes toward government, Citrin concluded that attitudes toward public services were "complex, and, on the whole, judicious . . . maintaining the status quo in most areas is the majority view" (1979, p. 128). He notes that citizens' general distrust of government is not reflected in attitudes toward specific services and policy objectives, about which survey respondents are typically more positive.

Exactly why citizens voted for Proposition 13 is ultimately less important than the consequences of that vote. The impacts of passage of the Jarvis-Gann Initiative were multiple: property taxes were cut, future revenue-raising constrained, and local governments made more dependent on the state.

Chapter 4 considers how California state and local governments responded to Proposition 13, and to its effects. Further California tax-reform measures, largely stimulated by Jarvis-Gann, will also be analyzed. Several follow-up initiatives appeared. Proposition 4, sponsored by Paul Gann, was approved by the electorate in November, 1979, and Proposition 9, sponsored by Howard Jarvis, was rejected in June, 1980. Other proposed tax-reform initiatives failed to qualify for the ballot. The legislature also enacted further tax relief, including one-time refunds, partial indexing of personal-income taxes, and abolition of the business-inventory tax. Any analysis of the ultimate impact of Proposition 13 must consider these reforms also. Some tax relief might have occurred in the absence of Jarvis-Gann, but given the past history of the California legislature, the pace, shape, and extent of tax reform would probably have been very different.

Appendix 3A:
Text of Proposition 13 (Addition of Article XIII-A to the California Constitution)

Section 1. a. The maximum amount of any ad valorem tax on real property shall not exceed One percent (1%) of the full cash value of such property. The one percent (1%) tax to be collected by the counties and apportioned according to law to the districts within the counties.

b. The limitation provided for in subdivision (a) shall not apply to ad valorem taxes or special assessments to pay the interest and redemption charges on any indebtedness approved by the voters prior to the time this section becomes effective.

Section 2. a. The full cash value means the County Assessors valuation of real property as shown on the 1975-76 tax bill under "full cash value," or thereafter, the appraised value of real property when purchased, newly constructed, or a change in ownership has occurred after the 1975 assessment. All real property not already assessed up to the 1975-76 tax levels may be reassessed to reflect that valuation.

b. The fair market value base may reflect from year to year the inflationary rate not to exceed two percent (2%) for any given year or reduction as shown in the consumer price index or comparable data for the area under taxing jurisdiction.

Section 3. a. From and after the effective date of this article, any changes in State taxes enacted for the purpose of increasing revenues collected pursuant thereto whether by increased rates or changes in methods of computation must be imposed by an Act passed by not less than two-thirds of all members elected to each of the two houses of the Legislature, except that no new ad valorem taxes on real property, or sales or transaction taxes on the sales of real property may be imposed.

Section 4. Cities, Counties, and special districts, by a two-thirds vote of the qualified electors of such district, may impose special taxes on such district, except ad valorem taxes on real property or a transaction tax or sales tax on the sale of real property within such City, County, or special district.

Section 5. This article shall take effect for the tax year beginning on July 1 following the passage of this Amendment except Section 3 which shall become effective upon the passage of this article.

Section 6. If any section, part, clause, or phrase hereof is for any reason held to be invalid or unconstitutional, the remaining sections shall not be affected but will remain in full force and effect.

Government in California: Adjusting to Fiscal Limits

Proposition 13 reduced property taxes available to local governments by $7 billion (60 percent of property-tax collections, equivalent to 22 percent of total local-governmental expenditures). A revenue reduction of this size in one year would be an exceptional event. But a cut of this magnitude did not occur. Despite preelection statements, Governor Brown and the legislature drew on the extraordinary state surplus that had accumulated over the previous three years to bail out local governments with $4.2 billion in assistance in FY 1978–1979. In July, 1979, a long-term local-government-financing package was passed, providing $4.8 billion in state assistance for FY 1979–1980. In FY 1980–1981, the state provided $5.3 billion in fiscal relief to local governments, and $6.0 billion in FY 1981–1982, which substantially revised the long-term framework adopted two years earlier.

Although the direct revenues of the state government were not affected by Jarvis-Gann, since the state receives no property-tax revenues, the state-level political system was immediately and dramatically affected. Indeed, the consequences of passage of the Jarvis-Gann Initiative were at least as great for the state political system as they were for California's local governments. There are three causes of this immediate and substantial impact. First, California, (as most states), acted as a major banker to local governments even before the tax revolt (Hamilton 1978a). The state collected statewide revenues, then appropriated, subventioned, and otherwise transferred approximately three-quarters of those monies to local governments. Second, the state had accumulated a substantial surplus (totaling $3.7 billion in June, 1978, an increase of nearly $2 billion that fiscal year), largely because of its income-elastic tax policies. Despite preelection pronouncements that no fiscal relief would be made available to local governments, substantial relief was quickly provided. Third, the political shockwaves of such an overwhelming rejection of the legislature's and governor's policy directions (culminating in the defeat of their alternative to Proposition 13) arrived immediately and remained strong.

This chapter examines the processes by which the intergovernmental fiscal system of California adjusted to the imposition of a sharp fiscal constraint. Most of the discussion emphasizes decisions made at the state level, particularly in the development of the fiscal-assistance, or bail-out packages

developed in each of the four budget cycles after June, 1978. In part, this
focus on the state level is the consequence of better data availability for that
level of government than for the several thousand units of local government. More fundamentally, decision making by the state was imperative
before local governments could respond to their new financial conditions.
The size and allocation of the fiscal assistance available from the state
affected their budgets powerfully. Equally important, their own-source
revenue bases and the constraints under which they could raise and allocate
funds were also modified by new state policies. Where data are available,
the changing fiscal circumstances of local governments are also analyzed.
These fiscal and related policy decisions were made in a highly charged
political environment, an environment in which additional tax-limiting initiatives were a distinct possibility, and other political issues competed for
legislators' attention. A parallel analysis of these political dynamics will
also often be included.

Three Cycles of State Response

A useful organizing framework for analysis of how the state of California
responded to Proposition 13 is to distinguish three cycles, in which certain
issues predominated. The first two periods correspond to legislative and
electoral cycles rather than to calendar or fiscal years. The first encompasses the period from passage of the initiative through the elections of
November, 1978; and the second covers the period from those general elections through the elections of June, 1980. The third cycle encompasses the
period from July, 1980 through June, 1981. Through these cycles, the state
response to Jarvis-Gann was becoming regularized, changing from a crisis-
dominated short cycle to a cycle that closely approximated the state's fiscal
year. From crisis-response to a normal budget process is one way of describing the story to be told by the analysis, although not a full portrayal of what
occurred. The dynamic that dominated state response attempted to somehow accommodate the discontinuity posed by fiscal constraint with the least
possible disruption of established processes.

The First Cycle: Quick Fiscal Response

In the three weeks between passage of the Jarvis-Gann Initiative and the
new fiscal year (July 1, 1978), the legislature developed its first-year, stop-
gap fiscal response (SB 154). David Doerr, Chief Consultant to the Assembly Revenue and Taxation Committee and key staff participant, provides a
first-hand account of the period (1979, pp. 1–3):

The pressures on legislators during those June days were fierce. Schools, cities, counties, and special districts were all vying for a larger share of limited resources—recognizing that what was allocated would be insufficient. Advocates of programs were seeking to have their programs fully protected by legislation, while local governments pleaded for maximum flexibility.

Local employee groups in each district made sure each member heard from home. From the other side, the self-proclaimed leaders of the revolution let it be known that they would not tolerate any tax increases, that they wanted "essential services maintained" but they wanted the "fat in government" cut.

The organization of the "bail-out" effort was critical. An unprecedented joint conference committee, comprised of the Legislative leadership of both houses was created. Senior Legislative staff were assigned to the Committee. Public input was received. Staff gathered data and prepared alternative strategies. Continual meetings were held by the party caucuses of each house for feedback. And a plan took shape.

It was decided to (1) define the key elements of the new property assessment procedure put into place by Proposition 13, (2) allocate the remaining property tax resources among local governments based on their historic share of the tax and (3) to provide enough additional resources to each government so that they would be "held harmful" to approximately 10 percent less revenue (from all sources) than projected for 1978–79 absent Proposition 13. This third objective, the so-called "bail-out," was accomplished by the state takeover of the funding of the SSI-SSP program, the Medi-Cal program and AFDC program and by the appropriation of block grant amounts to counties ($436 million), to cities ($250 million), to special districts (originally $125 million, but a total through subsequent bills of $192 million). From these amounts, there was subtracted one-third of any local reserves in excess of 5 percent of the local agency's 1977–78 revenues. In order to qualify for these funds, the Legislature required all jurisdictions to freeze employee salaries, a provision subsequently declared unconstitutional by the State Supreme Court.

To free up state revenues for the bail-out effort, the Legislature substantially reduced the then pending 1978–79 State budget. State general fund expenditures were held to $12.2 billion, a 4.3 percent increase over the $11.7 billion in 1977–78, the smallest percentage increase in the memory of most capital observers.

The politics of passing SB 154 were dominated by a perception of the necessity to provide at least a one-year transition period before the full effects of Proposition 13's revenue reductions were experienced. Edward K. Hamilton, an advisor to Governor Brown regarding the response to Proposition 13, reports that three key decisions shaped the ultimate legislation (1978b). First, the amount of state assistance had to be determined. Half, or $4 billion, of the estimated $8 billion to be available over the 1978–1979 and 1979–1980 fiscal years was chosen as a prudent yet substantial-enough sum to ease the transition. Second, the remaining property-tax revenues had to

be allocated. Recognition of the complexities involved in differential allocations, and the governor's refusal to discuss giving cities no allocation (suggested because cities have the greatest array of alternative revenue sources),
led to the ultimate prorata apportionment. Third, state assistance had to
be allocated. Here the availability of information concerning functions and
perceptions of state responsibility played a large role: education was seen as
an area of high state responsibility (prior to Proposition 13, state funds
totaled approximately 40 percent of statewide K–12 school expenditures),
much was known about school finances, and schools had few alternative
revenue sources. Health and welfare expenditures were largely mandated on
counties by the state, and good information was available concerning these
functions, particularly in large counties. The finances of cities were more
varied, information about such finances was poor, and cities were perceived
as having more alternative revenue sources. Finally, special districts were
multitudinous (over 4,000), and of mind-boggling variety. Few data were
available concerning their financing, and many legislators believed they
should be put under the control of general-purpose governments. The distribution of state assistance under SB 154 clearly reflected the consequences of
these orientations: schools and counties received 83 percent of the $4.2 bil-
lion in fiscal relief for FY 1978–1979; cities 6 percent; and special districts 3
percent. Table 4–1 reports the initial distributions of funds made under SB
154. In addition, an emergency-loan fund of $900 million was established to
be drawn upon by local jurisdictions with cash-flow problems; no such
loans were ever made.

Other issues were introduced into this debate, as analysts of political
processes suggest often occurs (Schattschneider 1960). Opponents of state
financial assistance for abortions succeeded in making reduction of funding
for abortions a condition of passage of the bail-out. Some Republican legislators sought unsuccessfully to place a revenue or expenditure limit on the
state. (In spite of the introduction of these other issues, the relatively narrow focus of debate on fiscal relief contrasted with a common legislative
strategy of seeking to advance policy proposals by amending them into
major, but unrelated, bills. Time pressures and the uncertainties of a vola-
tile political situation served to focus attention on the major task at hand.

One explanation for this devoted attention to the consequences of
Proposition 13 by a legislature that had foundered for a decade on the issue
of tax reform can be found in the then-upcoming November election, in
which the governorship, all of the Assembly seats and half of the Senate
seats would be on the ballot. Those elections were also a major factor in
spurring passage of a one-time, $1 billion income-tax rebate later in the
summer of 1978. A tax rebate had always been a possible use of the state
surplus, but it had not received serious consideration before passage of
Jarvis-Gann. As a condition for support of the June bail-out bill, Repub-

Table 4-1
State Assistance to Local Governments under SB 154, FY
1978-1979
(millions of dollars)

Type of Assistance	Amount
Cities (block grant)	250
Counties	
State assumption of mandated costs:	
Medi-Cal	418
SSI/SSP	168
AFDC	436
Food Stamp Administration	21
	1,044
Block grant assistance	436
Total to counties	1,480
Special districts (allocated by county boards of supervisors)	125
Special districts, "unmet needs" funds to be distributed by State Department of Finance	37
Public schools, K-12, block grant	2,000
County offices of education	65
Community colleges	240
Total state assistance	4,197

lican legislators had been promised that revenue or expenditure limits would be considered later that summer. When no agreement on expenditure lids could be reached, the one-time tax rebate emerged as politically desirable. The bill that was ultimately passed and signed rebated $675 million of 1978 income taxes (by reducing tax liability for that year) and created temporary, partial indexing of state income-tax brackets (inflation greater than 3 percent was offset). In addition, the bill provided for a once-in-a-lifetime exclusion of up to $100,000 in capital gains received upon sale of a residence and provided a special tax credit for senior citizens. The penchant before Proposition 13 for redistributive tax relief still existed, although weakened.

This preelection positioning was largely effective. Jerry Brown won reelection as governor by a larger plurality than that of his initial election, helped not only by a lackluster campaign by Republican candidate Evelle Younger, the State Attorney general, but also by Brown's strong commitment to implementation of Proposition 13. Indeed, he earned the epithet of "Jerry Jarvis" in the eyes of some who opposed his policies. Most vocal in this regard were state employees for whom Brown proposed no salary increases in his revised FY 1978–1979 budget. Being loudly booed at summer gatherings of the California State Employees' Association added considerable credence to Brown's campaign to be perceived as a tax-cutter.

Not all candidates for reelection were so fortunate. Aided partly by direct mailings bearing computerized "personal" messages from Howard Jarvis, several challenges to incumbents were successful. Of the Assembly incumbents seeking reelection, six Democrats were defeated; in the Senate, two incumbent Democrats were defeated. This rate of defeats is high, suggesting an episodic wave of voter dissatisfaction with incumbents.

The Second Cycle: Institutionalizing Responses and
New Fiscal Constraints

In the second cycle after passage of Proposition 13, the state enacted a plan for long-term fiscal relief for local governments, passed legislation to "clean up" various ambiguities in Proposition 13 (most notably those concerning assessment practices), institutionalized procedures for closer monitoring of revenues and expenditures, and adopted full, though still temporary, indexing of the state personal-income tax. A "Spirit of 13" expenditure-limit initiative (Proposition 4, developed by Paul Gann) was adopted by the electorate in the November, 1979 election and Jarvis II ("Jaws II" to its opponents) qualified for the June, 1980 ballot but was defeated. Broadly perceived, public institutions sought long-term accommodation to Proposition 13 during this period while the organizers of tax-revolt-oriented initiatives sought further victories.

Developing legislation to follow SB 154 was the major issue confronting the California legislature in its 1979 session. A long-term bill was ultimately passed, after much contention. Governor Brown vacillated on the choice between a long-term plan and a second one-year bail-out, at first sympathetic to a long-term bill, then arguing that another one-year bill was all that was possible, ultimately signing AB 8, the long-term bill. Assembly Speaker Leo McCarthy strongly and consistently advocated a long-term approach. Governor Brown's initial long-term proposal, which gave all of the remaining property-tax revenues to the schools, was not seriously considered by the legislature. Similarly, McCarthy's first proposal, which took sales-tax revenues away from cities and counties, received scant attention. Following the procedure used in developing SB 154, a Joint Conference Committee made up of three members of the Assembly and three of the Senate was created to provide an arena for resolution of this issue.

Assemblyman Leroy F. Greene served as committee chairman, and his AB 8, originally a school-finance bill, became the vehicle for development of a long-term local-government financial system. In addition to being a long-term as opposed to a one-year bill, AB 8 differed from SB 154 in other critical dimensions. It was a much more complex bill, 108 pages in length (compared with 50 pages for SB 154), included not only matters relating directly to the fiscal relations between local governments and the state, but also covered extraneous issues such as increased state contributions to the state-run teachers' retirement fund. SB 154 had constrained local governments' allocation of funds to activities through such devices as giving priority to police and fire expenditures; AB 8 eschewed such mandates but did empower the Auditor General to audit local-government financial transactions. Finally, because the capability of the state budget to accommodate projected expenditures in the indefinite future was uncertain, a deflator clause was added that would reduce state assistance to local governments should the state's revenues fall below estimates. The deflator clause would reduce local-government fiscal assistance by the amount that state revenues fell below a 1979–1980 base level, adjusted annually for increases in the Consumer Price Index and in population of the state. However, when the state's ability to give assistance was limited, as in preparing the FY 1981–1982 budget, the deflator mechanism was suspended.

Some continuities existed between SB 154 and AB 8. Abortion funding was again an issue, delaying passage of AB 8 until satisfactory resolution could be found in the state budget, which was being enacted contemporaneously. The same priority of claimants for state assistance was carried forward; schools and counties received more generous allocations than did cities and special districts.

Tables 4–2 and 4–3 provide information on the fiscal features of AB 8. Table 4–2 contrasts the cost of SB 154 (FY 1978–1979) to appropriations for the first year for AB 8 (FY 1979–1980) and projections for the second year under AB 8 (FY 1980–1981). The complexity of the transfers of fiscal assistance to different types of local government is apparent in this table. Nominal state assistance for education, shown by the stub-column entry "Net fiscal relief, education," increased by 15 percent, and nominal state assistance for the health and welfare activities of counties increased 21 percent. These numbers have little meaning without relationship to the effects of the termination of block grants to cities, counties, and special districts, and to the reduction in business-inventory tax-exemption reimbursement ($17 million to counties and $21 million to cities), shown in the bottom third of table 4–2.

Full understanding of the fiscal relief afforded local government under AB 8 is not possible without the information provided in table 4–3 concerning redistribution of property-tax revenues from schools to counties, cities, and special districts. The overriding decision-making rule used by the legislature was that total revenues going to each type of local jurisdiction should

Table 4-2
General-Fund Cost Summary of SB 154 and AB 8
(millions of dollars)

Cost	1978–1979	1979–1980	1980–1981
School Finance			
K-12			
Revenue limit	6,370	6,800	7,252
STRS	144	144	168
Categoricals and other	959	1,159	1,234
Total, K-12	7,473	8,103	8,654
County superintendents	276	319	361
Community Colleges	1,141	1,226	1,321
Total cost	8,890	9,648	10,336
Less local share	−2,507	−1,913	−2,085
State share	6,383	7,735	8,251
Less amount in budget	−3,927	−4,147	−4,271
Fiscal relief, education	2,456	3,588	3,880
Replacement of property tax			
shifted to other local governments	0	757	823
Net fiscal relief, education	2,456	2,831	3,057
Health and Welfare			
AFDC			
Family payments	244	204	231
BHI payments	79	100	115
Administration	85	0	0
SSI/SSP	182	200	218
Food Stamp Administration	22	0	0
Medi-Cal	459	505	550
County health services	0	267	286
Waiver of state hospital match	0	6	0
Other	0	17	18
Net fiscal relief, health and welfare	1,071	1,299	1,418
Block grants			
Counties	436	0	0
Cities	250	0	0
Special districts	190	0	0
Total block grants	876	0	0
Reduction in BIE Reimbursement			
Counties	0	17	0
Cities	0	21	0
Total fiscal relief[a]	4,401	4,849	5,298

Source: Legislature, State of California, *Conference Committee Report* (Sacramento: State of California, 1979).

[a]Does not include $14 million in funds previously appropriated by SB 154 to be released to cities under redefinition of reserves (AB 227).

Table 4-3
Property-Tax Redistribution 1979-1980
(millions of dollars)

	Schools	Counties	Cities	Special Districts
1978-1979 Property-tax revenues[a]	2,409	1,349	448	362
Estimated 1979-1980 property-tax revenues before redistribution	2,670	1,475	493	398
Revenue redistribution: amount transferred to replace block grants	-908	+480	+228	+200
Reduction in state reimbursement for inventory exemption (1979-1980 only)		-17	-21	
Amount transferred to replace reduction in AFDC buy-outs	-116	+116		
Amount transferred to offset new state support for county health programs[a]	+267	-267		
Net transfer	-757	+312	+207	+200
Estimated 1979-1980 revenues after redistribution[b]	1,913	1,787	700	598

Source: Legislature, State of California, *Conference Committee Report* (Sacramento: State of California, 1979).

[a]Includes state subventions for tax relief but excludes debt-service levies.

[b]These figures are for the new property tax *base* under AB 8; local governments receive in property taxes each year an amount equal to the prior year's base, plus revenues from assessed value growth on "situs" (location of new construction or changes in ownership).

be controlled so that each type would have roughly equal total revenue reduction or growth. To this end, the legislature in AB 8 allocated not only state assistance, but also a property-tax *base,* dramatically affecting local governments' own-source revenues, a large part of which consisted of the property tax despite Proposition 13.

Indeed, a major policy issue confronted by the state in making decisions regarding fiscal assistance to local governments was how much to allow these revenues from the property tax to increase without decreasing state aid. In spite of Proposition 13, assessed values, and hence property-tax revenues, increased at a rate greater than 10 percent annually, causing the state to fear that it would be in the position of sending fiscal assistance to jurisdictions whose revenues were increasing more rapidly than its own.

This issue reemerged even more strongly in deliberations on the FY 1981–1982 state budget and fiscal-relief package.

Another dimension of the fiscal relief/own-source revenue conundrum concerned the impact of alternative policies on local-government decisions about new development, a process local jurisdictions control more directly than does the state because they possess most of the land-use regulatory powers. A major flaw of SB 154 was that it did not return increased property-tax revenues to jurisdictions in which new construction occurred. Faced with the high probability of increased expenditures to provide services for new development without compensating new revenues, jurisdictions hesitated to allow development. AB 8 sought to remedy this weakness of SB 154 by assigning increased property-tax revenues (created by new construction, transfer of ownership, or the 2 percent annual increases allowed by Proposition 13) on a situs basis to the jurisdictions in which new development occurred. This matter of financing the capital infrastructure required by new development and extending additional services necessitated by such development was not fully resolved.

At a more technical level, the implementation of Proposition 13 required sweeping changes in property-assessment practices. A market-value-based system was replaced with a "base-value-plus-adjustments" system. Legal and technical questions that required resolution before full transition to the post-Proposition 13 system concerned definition of the 1975 base, change of ownership, and new construction. Millions of dollars of tax liabilities and revenues rode on these decisions, yet the language of the Jarvis-Gann Initiative and related constitutional and statutory provisions was ambiguous in these aspects. Some issues were decided in the courts (for example, that the unsecured property roll was controlled by Proposition 13). But most of the questions were resolved legislatively through two clean-up bills, AB 1488 and AB 1019. In general, the definitions and interpretations adopted in these bills favored taxpayers as opposed to tax collectors. For example, transfer of an interest in a property by a partner is treated as equivalent to sale of stock in a corporation; change of ownership (and reassessment to full market value) occurs only when the partnership itself ceases to have immediate beneficial use of the property. As another example, when alteration of an existing structure is substantial, it qualifies as new construction, to be assessed at full market value, but does not trigger reassessment of the preexisting structure or the underlying land. Undoubtedly, hesitation to tamper with the popular initiative should be given some of the credit for this posture, but the decisions are also reasonable in terms of their technical attributes (ease of application) and their balancing of secondary economic effects (such as not discouraging property improvement).

Beyond specific adjustments to Proposition 13, broader institutional modifications were also adopted during this second cycle. The most formalized among these was creation of a new Commission on State Finance. Carried by State Senate President Pro Tem James Mills and supported by State Treasurer Jesse Unruh, the commission, composed of four legislators and three members of the executive branch, was to provide quarterly estimates of general-fund revenues, expenditures, and surplus levels. The commission has an executive officer, a small staff and a FY 1981-1982 budget of $505,345. It is intended to rely in part on existing legislative and executive-branch support, and is subject to a 1984 sunset provision under which it is terminated unless reauthorized by the legislature. Although the major impetus behind the creation of the commission was the desire to avoid the surprises and political embarrassments of fluctuating surplus estimates (usually too low) characteristic since 1974, the commission's June estimates were to provide the trigger for the deflator clause of AB 8. A less formal, but still important response could be seen in the types and quality of fiscal analyses undertaken by some legislative committees. As would be expected, the "money" committees in the Assembly and the Senate (Senate Finance, Assembly Revenue and Taxation Committees) were the locus of this effort. Passage of Propositions 13 and 4 and the prospect of Proposition 9 encouraged more extensive and careful analyses of the California public sector. Particularly noteworthy was the clear recognition of interdependence of state and local government finances.

A final institutional accommodation to the spirit, if not the requirements, of Proposition 13 was the full indexing of the California personal-income tax and abolition of the business-inventory tax. The partial-indexing bill was passed before the November, 1978 elections. A year later, in the summer of 1979, full indexing was achieved by extending tax brackets by the final 3 percent excluded in the earlier bill. However, this measure is subject to a 1982 sunset provision, after which partial indexing will continue. Reduction of property taxation on business inventories had been a legislative objective since 1968, and increasing exemptions passed periodically since that time (15 percent in 1968; 30 percent in 1971; 50 percent in 1974-1975). The state replaced the revenues lost to local-property-taxing jurisdictions. Contemporaneously with the indexing of the personal-income tax, the business-inventory tax was totally repealed, but provision was made for annual increases in the corporate-income-tax rate (AB 66).

Although the legislature was still seeking accommodation to dislocations caused by Proposition 13, more fiscal limits were on the horizon. Proposition 4, the "Spirit-of-13" expenditure limit sponsored by Paul Gann, was overwhelmingly approved in the November, 1979 election, substantially surpassing the plurality achieved by Proposition 13 (76 percent compared with 65 percent "yes" votes). A proposed initiative to abolish the state sales tax failed to qualify. But Howard Jarvis' second initiative, Proposition 9, the prinicipal effects of which were to fully index personal-income-tax brackets and halve personal-income-tax rates, qualified for the June, 1980 ballot.

Whereas Proposition 13 cut the property-tax rate and changed assessment practices to a base-period-plus-limited-adjustments method, Proposition 4 imposed a limit on overall expenditures, an approach favored by some commentators because it preserved more flexibility in governmental decision making. Proposition 4 had six major provisions:

1. Appropriations to state and local governments from tax sources are limited to a formula based on changes in population and the cost of living (Consumer Price Index). Growth of per-capita personal income is used to adjust the limit if this figure is less than CPI.
2. The limitation may be adjusted temporarily by a majority vote of the electors.
3. Tax revenues in excess of the limit must be returned to the taxpayers within two years.
4. The state is required to reimburse local governments for new programs or higher levels of service that it mandates.
5. Fees and charges in excess of the cost of providing the service are within and controlled by the limit.
6. Provisions are made for emergencies, for government debt service, for new entities of government, and for transfers of functions from one entity to another or from a tax source to a fee.

As in Proposition 13, ambiguity exists in Proposition 4 concerning certain key definitions, although this initiative appears to have fewer such issues than does the earlier property-tax limit. A useful exploration of these issues is provided by the State of California Legislative Analyst (1979). This publication also provides a schematic detailing of the operation of the limit for the state, reproduced in figure 4–1 (1979, p. 4).

Operation of Proposition 4 in regard to local governments follows similar calculations. The initiative provides important incentives for use of nontax revenues (such as user fees up to the cost of service provision) and generally encourages much more careful attention to cost accounting. A particularly important case of this general incentive concerns state-mandated local-government expenditures, which must be reimbursed by the state and included within the state limit, while excluded from the local-government limit.

Projection of the operation of the limit (which did not become operational until FY 1980–1981) is made difficult by the distinction between

Total Income of State

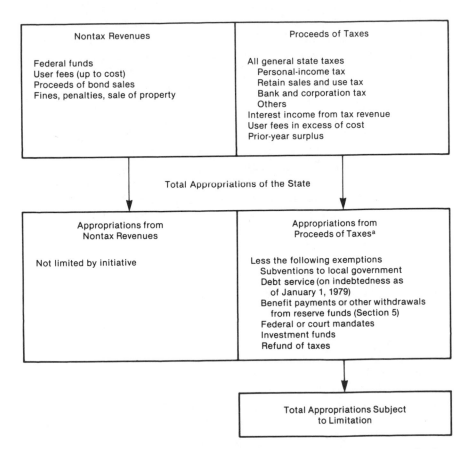

Source: Legislative Analyst, State of California, *An Analysis of Proposition 4, the Gann "Spirit of 13" Initiative* (Sacramento: Legislative Analyst, 1979).

[a]Any proceeds of taxes *not* appropriated (that is, surplus funds) would be subject to section 2 of the initiative, which requires that surplus funds be returned to the people.

Figure 4-1. Determining "Appropriations Subject to Limitation" for State Government under Proposition 4

limited and nonlimited appropriations. For example, $8.3 billion of the state's FY 1978–1979 appropriations of $14.2 billion were subject to limit. Moreover, the limit may be adjusted, for a maximum of four years, by a vote of the people, and may be surpassed by a one-year "emergency," provided that appropriation limits for the following three years are reduced to prevent an aggregate increase in expenditures. The governor's budget for

FY 1980–1981 projected appropriations of $16.0 billion, well below the limit of $16.8 billion. Some analysts believe that the limit would rarely be operational; others forecast the limit will be reached within the near future.

Passage of Proposition 9 in the June, 1980 elections would have made the limit moot for several years. That measure would have reduced state revenues by $1.8 to 3.8 billion for FY 1980–1981 and by $3.6 to 4.0 billion for FY 1981–1982, depending on how the state (and the courts) implemented Proposition 9 (Rodda 1980, pp. 1–13). A revenue reduction of this size is beyond what anyone believed could be handled through the AB 8 deflator. Senator Rodda, chairman of the Senate Finance Committee, anticipated that an extraordinary process would again be invoked by the legislature (Rodda 1980). The model immediately at hand, of course, was the kind of joint committee that developed SB 154 and AB 8. The substantive proposal Rodda viewed as most feasible would entail reducing AB-8 appropriations by 50 percent and all other state-budget appropriations by "appropriate" percentages, averaging 15 percent across the board (Rodda 1980, pp. 30–31). Proposition 9 was defeated, however, obviating the need for extensive budget reductions.

The election campaigns for and against Propositions 4 and 9, when contrasted with one another and with the Proposition-13 campaign, illustrate how the California political establishment sought accommodation to the fiscal-limits movement. As discussed earlier, with the exception of a very few Republican legislators, virtually all California state and local public officials opposed Proposition 13. Proposition 4, in sharp contrast, was supported by many public officials. Speaker of the Assembly Leo McCarthy and Assembly Minority Leader Carol Hallett (R) joined Paul Gann in writing the argument in favor of Proposition 4 included in the official ballot pamphlet sent to all voters. The opposition statement was signed by Jonathan C. Lewis, Executive Director, California Tax Reform Association (which advocated tax reforms that would shift tax burdens from individuals to businesses and commerical interests); Susan F. Rice, president, League of California Voters; and John F. Henning, Executive Secretary-Treasurer, California Labor Federation, AFL-CIO. Governor Brown endorsed the measure before the election, as did Lieutenant Governor Mike Curb, a Republican. Some commentators observed that most elected officials supported Proposition 4 because they believed it would win regardless of their positions. They doubted that it would affect government revenues and expenditures very much, because the limit could grow with population and personal income, and they also discerned loopholes in the measure such as ability to impose fees and charges for service, opportunities for base-year loading, and exclusion of federal and court mandates from the limit (Fitzgerald 1979). No organized campaign was ever mounted against Proposition 4. The only substantial expenditure against it was $10,000 spent by the state AFL-CIO for radio advertising. Proponents spent over $1,250,000 in support of Proposition 4, probably the most lopsided expenditure pattern ever for an initiative. Only 8 percent of the contributions to the campaign for Proposition 13 were $1,000 or more. Although 19 percent of the contributions in support of Proposition 4 were of that magnitude, the initiative attracted many small contributions, testimony to its appeal (FPPC 1979).

Proposition 9, ("Jaws II" to its opponents), stimulated a much more hotly contested campaign. Proposition 9 was qualified in a distinctive manner, "without human hands," by direct mail. Butcher-Forde, the public-relations firm working with Jarvis, developed an impressive technology for qualifying initiatives. Working from lists of signatures on the qualifying petition for Proposition 13 and lists of contributors to that campaign, plus sophisticated stratifications of voter-registration lists by census-tract characteristics, Butcher-Forde mailed out 6 million pieces of mail on Proposition 9. Each envelope contained a qualifying petition, a solicitation of contributions to the campaign, and a letter from Jarvis extolling the importance of the initiative, referring (as the mail campaign progressed) to a specific individual on the addressee's block or nearby who had both signed the qualifying petition and contributed to the campaign. The 400,000 responses contained 820,000 signatures on qualifying petitions, half again as many as needed, including 200,000 contributions. The campaign to *qualify* Proposition 9 cost just over $2 million, of which only $6,000 was raised in contributions of $1,000 or more (FPPC 1980). Most of the balance apparently was derived from the direct-mail campaign.

After qualifying Proposition 9, its supporters raised and spent another $1 million campaigning for its approval in the June, 1980 election. But during this campaign they were outspent by the opponents of Proposition 9. In the critical last two months before the election, opponents outspent advocates by a two-to-one margin, raising most of their funds from public-employee unions and organizations. In contrast to the general support (or at least silence) of elected officials for Proposition 4, Proposition 9 was opposed by virtually all Democratic state-level elected officials and most local officials, receiving support only from some Republican officials (such as Carol Hallet, Assembly Minority Leader). Opponents argued that the California public sector could not afford the $5 billion reduction in revenue that would result (personal-income-tax rates would be halved, full indexing for inflation made permanent and the business-inventory tax fully abolished), and that the wealthy would benefit most from the tax cuts. Proponents argued that Proposition 9 would stimulate the economy (Arthur Laffer publically supported the initiative on this basis) and reduce waste in government.

Proposition 9 began with a favorable evaluation in the polls, but a negative evaluation followed quite quickly, as shown in table 4–4. Citizens

Table 4–4
Polled Attitudes toward Proposition 9
(percentages)

Poll Date	Know Specifics of Proposition 9	In Favor	Against	No Opinion
February 1980	40	54	34	12
April 1980	61	43	48	9
May 1980	80	38	52	10

Source: February and April polls are California polls reported in: *San Francisco Chronicle,* February 29, 1980, and *Napa Register,* April 14, 1980. May poll was reported in the *Los Angeles Times,* May 11, 1980.

were less dissatisfied with the income tax than they had been with the property tax before passage of Proposition 13 (49 percent said the income tax was a fair tax as opposed to 44 percent who said it was unfair); many (40 percent) believed Proposition 9 would lead to increases in other taxes; and 37 percent of those who reported that they had voted for Proposition 13 told the May *Los Angeles Times* poll that they intended to vote no on Proposition 9 (May 11, 1980). Proposition 9 was rejected in the June, 1980 election with 61 percent of the electorate voting no on the measure.

The defeat of Proposition 9 ended (at least through 1981) the era of initiative-instigated fiscal limits in California. Proposition 13 and 4 had been approved, but Proposition 9 had been defeated, and the Campos Initiative, which would have abolished the sales tax, a major source of state and local revenue, had failed to garner sufficient signatures to qualify for the ballot. The threat had been real and substantial, as shown in table 4–5, which calculates the "worst-case" scenario for state and local revenues had Proposition 9 passed and the Campos Initiative qualified and passed.

After Proposition 9 was defeated, Governor Brown and the legislature moved to ease the fiscal constraints imposed on state and local governments in the previous months. On June 30, after the defeat of Jarvis II, but just before the end of the fiscal year, legislation was passed and signed that used a bookkeeping device to prevent a $334-million-dollar rebate required under Proposition 4. Later in that summer, further legislation was enacted to forestall any local governments from rebating $300 million in windfall revenues received when the state Supreme Court ruled that Proposition 13 did not apply immediately to unsecured property (machinery, leases, boats, and so on) on local-government tax rolls. In September, Governor Brown signed two more bills lessening the impact of Proposition 4. One allowed San Francisco to use the population-growth figure for the entire nine-county San-Francisco-Bay area in computing its revenue limit, based on the argument

Table 4-5
A Worst-Case Scenario for California State- and Local-Government Revenues
(billions of dollars)

Projected Changes in	Local Governments	State (General Fund)
FY 1977–1978 (actual)	25.4	13.5
FY 1978–1979 (budgeted, includes $4.2 billion in state aid)	25.0	15.7
Gann Initiative (Proposition 4)[a]	− 3.4	− 2.2
Jarvis Initiative (Propostion 9)[b]	—	− 5,0
Campos Initiative[c]	− 1.3	− 6.4
State aid to localities[d]	− 4.2	+ 4.2
Net revenues:	16.1	6.3

Sources: FY 1977–1978 and FY 1978–1979 figures for local governments from State of California, Department of Finance (January, 1979); for state general fund, Governor's Budget for FY 1979–1980 (January, 1979).

[a]Legislative Analyst's estimate of $6 billion reduction by FY 1983–1984, apportioned pro rata to local and state governments.

[b]Estimate of the first-year impacts of Proposition 9.

[c]Estimated by eliminating sales-tax revenues projected in the Governor's Budget, January 1979.

[d]Adjustment based on assumption that had Proposition 9 and the Campos Initiatives passed, the state would have terminated the fiscal assistance to local governments enacted after Proposition 13 passed.

that even if the population of San Francisco were declining, it still incurred expenditure obligations from the commuters living in outlying counties but working in San Francisco. The second bill was more complex, defining state aid to schools in such a manner that is was excluded from the revenue limit, tying the school-revenue limit to changes in total population rather than enrollments, and allowing local governments to establish new fees for services such as garbage collection without reducing their revenue limits in return (*Los Angeles Times,* September 30, 1980).

Stimulated by the campaign for Proposition 9, the legislature had overwhelmingly passed a bill permanently and fully indexing the personal-income tax in the spring of 1980, a bill that would have made permanent the full indexing adopted in the fall of 1979, but included a sunset provision reinstating partial indexing after 1982. After the defeat of Proposition 9, Governor Brown vetoed this bill, and the legislature failed twice to override his veto. Brown argued that full and permanent indexing was too costly when the state faced an uncertain fiscal future. In one regard, the state's fiscal future was not uncertain: it was consuming the accumulated surplus, annually expending more than current revenues. Dealing with this exhaustion of the surplus dominated the third cycle of state response to Proposition 13.

The Third Cycle: Confronting the Exhaustion of the Surplus

Deliberations on the FY 1980–1981 and FY 1981–1982 state budgets were dominated by the impending exhaustion of the state surplus, that accumulation of funds that had allowed the state to bail out local governments after passage of Proposition 13. Table 4–6 presents one analysis of this exhaustion; other analyses varied slightly, but presented the same general picture. FY 1981–1982 was widely believed to be the year in which the effects of Proposition 13 would really occur.

Early deliberations on the FY 1980–1981 state budget were overshadowed by the possibility that Proposition 9 might pass and dramatically alter the fiscal choices available. After the defeat of Proposition 9, the most debated issues in the budget became the cost-of-living increases for state employees, welfare recipients, and health-care providers (Salzman 1980). A drawn-out debate on these issues ensued consisting largely of political posturing. Legislative approval of a budget bill did not occur until July 16, a record tardiness beyond the constitutional budget deadline of June 15, and more than two weeks past the start of the new fiscal year on July 1. The package of local fiscal assistance followed the format established by AB 8 in 1979: $923 million in property-tax revenues were shifted from schools to other local governments; counties received $1,472 million in health-and-welfare buy-outs; and schools received $3,048 million; totaling $5.4 billion.

The FY 1981–1982 budget cycle got off to a shaky start when Governor Brown proposed a state budget that was quickly judged unacceptable by the legislature, which then had the task of developing an alternative. Reflecting its organizational structure, the legislature developed four alternative budgets: one each for Assembly and Senate Democrats and Republicans. Since the accumulated surplus that had eased budget making in the three previous budget cycles was now exhausted, each of the five proposed budgets entailed substantial revisions in previous policies. As an example, Governor Brown's budget proposal suspended statuatory cost-of-living adjustments for 1981–1982, shifted a portion of the property tax from cities and counties back to schools, reduced state programs below the existing service base, and recaptured about $500 million in unsecured property-tax revenues freed by court decision that would have otherwise gone to local government.

Early agreement on the size of the cost-of-living increase for welfare recipients set the stage for relatively harmonious bipartisan work on the budget, culminating in a two-house conference committee that met for a

Table 4-6
Fluctuation in the State General-Fund Surplus, FY 1973-1974 to FY 1981-1982
(billions of dollars)

Annual and Cumulative Balances	*End of Fiscal Year*								
	1973-1974	*1974-1975*	*1975-1976*	*1976-1977*	*1977-1978*	*1978-1979*	*1979-1980*	*1980-1981*	*1981-1982*
Annual balance, current revenues less current expenditures	-0.4	+0.2	+0.1	+0.5	+1.9	-1.0	-0.9	-1.4	-1.3
Accumulated surplus	+0.2	+0.4	+0.6	+1.6	+3.7	+2.7	+1.8	+0.4	-0.9

Source: Calculations by Albert S. Rodda, Chairman, Senate Finance Committee, *Fiscal Implications of Jarvis II for the State of California and Agencies of California Local Government, Including the Schools, As Viewed From the Perspective of a Practical Politician* (Sacramento: Senate Finance Committee, 1980).

seven-day marathon session to resolve 1,500 differences in the Senate and Assembly budget bills. The budget enacted authorized $22.7 billion in general-fund expenditures, a 2.0 percent increase over the FY 1980–1981 budget. When special funds (FY 1981–1982 budget of $3.8 billion, up 8.9 percent) and bonds (FY 1981–1982 budget of $296 million, up 47.9 percent) were added, total expenditures authorized were $25.8 billion, an increase of 3.4 percent (State of California, Legislative Analyst July, 1981).

Among the policy changes required to fit budgeted FY 1981–1982 expenditures within the limit of available revenues were a reduction in cost-of-living increases for welfare recipients to 9.2 percent from the 11 percent projected in previous statutes; a limit in cost increases of health-care providers to 6 percent; transferral of $390.6 million from the Tidelands Oil Fund (previously used for capital projects, largely for higher education) to the general fund; reduction of fiscal relief to cities and counties by $221.8 million from what it would have been under AB 8 (the long-term fiscal-relief bill adopted in 1979); and a slight reduction in budgeted personnel years in state government (-0.2 percent). Among increased expenditures was a 31.3-percent increase in funding for the legislature itself (to $105 million). This increase was required to fund the additional staff promised in the recent battles for leadership positions, especially in the Assembly.

Fiscal assistance to local government was handled somewhat differently than in previous years. However, the relief package developed and the process used were essentially logical extensions of previous patterns. Maintaining expenditure levels in K–12 schools had been the highest priority of the legislature in developing previous fiscal-assistance packages (SB 154 and AB 8). Second priority was historically given to county health-and-welfare functions and last priority to cities. In deliberations on the FY 1981–1982 budget, no single local-government fiscal-relief act was developed. There was no equivalent to SB 154 or AB 8 of 1979. As reported by the Legislative Analyst (1981, p. 8–9) seven bills related to the Budget Act (SB 110) structured the fiscal future of California local governments for FY 1981–1982:

1. *SB 633, (Chapter 69, Statutes of 1981).* This act made numerous changes to expenditures in the health and welfare areas. In the welfare area, SB 633: provided a 9.2 percent cost-of-living adjustment (COLA) for AFDC, SSI/SSP, and IHSS recipients; restricted eligibility for the state AFDC-U program; eliminated AFDC aid to 18–21 year-olds attending school; and eliminated the Aid to the Partially Self-Supporting Blind Program. In the health area it: reinstated a county match for alcohol, drug, and mental health programs; and established a sliding fee schedule for family-planning services.

2. *AB 777, (Chapter 100, Statutes of 1981):* AB 777 authorized the major funding increases for K–12 school districts and county offices of education. Specifically, it provided an 8 percent cost-of-living adjustment

(COLA) for apportionments, a 7.2 percent COLA for county offices of education, a 102 percent minimum-revenue guarantee, and additional transportation funds. The Budget Act contained sufficient resources to fund the costs of AB 777.

3. *SB 102, (Chapter 101, Statutes of 1981).* This act contained a number of provisions affecting local governments. SB 102 suspended the AB 8 deflator for one year, permanently eliminated three subventions for a general-fund revenue gain of $58 million in 1981-1982 and reduced the motor-vehicle license fee subvention on a one-time basis for a revenue gain of $114 million. It also redirected to the state 85 percent of the county share and 100 percent of the city share of the additional 1978-1979 unsecured property taxes resulting from a recent Supreme Court decision, by transferring these amounts from cities and counties to school districts. The act also redirected to the state the interest earned by local governments on the unsecured property-tax collections. It did this by reducing business-inventory subventions by $50 million.

4. *AB 251, (Chapter 102, Statutes of 1981).* This act made statutory changes required by the budget. Specifically, it revised the method of delivering Medi-Cal services, limited school meals, and modified day-care licensing. It also contained eight appropriations that were later repealed by AB 250, Chapter 133, Statutes of 1981, and inserted into SB 840.

5. *AB 1626, (Chapter 103, Statutes of 1981).* AB 1626 established a financing mechanism for community-college state aid for fiscal years 1981-1982 and 1982-1983. It provided a 5 percent COLA, allowed growth in average daily attendance (ADA), and continued special-equity funding for districts with certain enrollment patterns and expenditure characteristics. With some modifications, AB 1626 extended the provisions of current law as contained in AB 8.

6. *AB 250, (Chapter 133, Statutes of 1981).* In addition to repealing the AB 251 appropriations, AB 250 made technical corrections to SB 102 and AB 777.

7. *SB 840, (Chapter 169, Statutes of 1981).* SB 840 is the major clean-up bill for the budget. It included $139 million in appropriations that were inappropriately included in AB 251. The largest of these appropriations was $125 million for tax refunds related to the Unsecured Property Tax. SB 840 also made numerous technical corrections to SB 110.

Five separate major bills (SB 633, AB 777, SB 102, AB 251, AB 1626) and two clean-up bills (AB 250 and SB 840), plus the relevant sections of the budget bill (SB 110) itself, were used to structure local-government financing for FY 1981-1982; legislative deliberations linked the bills in a way that was suggestive of their evolving orientation to the bail-out.

Whatever relief was provided had to fit into the overall framework of revenues available to the state. Importantly, in a further extension of the precedent established with AB 8 (1979), local-government own-source revenues were included in this calculation of total available revenues. In particular, growth in property-tax revenues was considered essentially equivalent to new state revenue, to be allocated among all local governments or used to offset state assistance. As assessed values of property increased by 17.8 percent in 1980–1981, resulting in equivalent growth in property-tax revenues in FY 1981–1982, almost double the rate (9.7 percent) that state general-fund revenues are expected to increase in the same fiscal year, state officials felt fully justified in considering this factor when developing their budget and its allocations of fiscal assistance to local governments. The governor's proposed budget shifted $420 million in regular property-tax revenues from cities and counties to education. The budget enacted achieved much the same effect by the provisions of SB 102, as described.

But the most important attribute of the FY 1981–1982 budget process in the evolving response to Proposition 13 was the extent to which there was no longer a separate bail-out and to which decisions had been incorporated into the state's normal annual budget cycle. That budget cycle was now undeniably somewhat more complex, but the shift from extraordinary bail-out measures to regularized budget processes had largely been accomplished. Symptomatically, unified analyses of the total local fiscal-relief package of the sort presented in table 4–2 were missing from legislative deliberations in the spring of 1981. Though initial analyses of the governor's budget included how his proposals differed from those projected under AB 8, by the end of the process *no* unified analysis of the impact of the budget and related bills on local governments was available in public documents. Instead, the Legislative Analyst (1981) used three separate tables to report what had occurred. Table 4–7 reproduces its comparison of the allocations to cities, counties, and special districts with those of FY 1980–1981. Missing from this table are allocations for K–12 education and community colleges, for which data are provided in table 4–8.

An examination of these two tables shows that the biases that the state legislature exhibited in the first bail-out, SB 154, and continued in the long-term fiscal-assistance bill, AB 8, again dominated policymaking. Elementary and secondary education received state aid and property taxes were shifted sufficiently to increase their revenues 11.4 percent. The health-and-welfare buy-out assistance to counties increased 10.8 percent. The two areas of highest state priority fared well again in FY 1981–1982. Special districts also did relatively well, receiving an increase of 11.5 percent in property-tax revenues that had been shifted to them under AB 8. Counties lost 85 percent of the property taxes received on unsecured property ($69.6 million) and cities lost 100 percent of those funds ($152.2 million).

Table 4-7
Local Fiscal Relief, FY 1980-1981 and 1981-1982
(millions of dollars)

			Difference	
Jurisdiction	1980–1981	1981–1982	Amount	Percentage
Cities				
AB 8 property-tax shift from schools	278.0	310.0		
Less SB 102 reduction	—	− 152.2		
Total, cities	278.0	157.8	− 120.2	− 43.2
Counties				
Health and welfare buy-outs				
County health services	313.6	338.4	24.8	7.9
Medi-Cal	573.6	639.6	66.0	11.5
SSI/SSP	235.0	262.0	27.0	11.5
AFDC	368.4	412.2	43.8	12.9
Total, health and welfare buy-outs	1,490.6	1,652.2	161.6	10.8
AB 8 property-tax shift from schools	398.0	443.8		
Less SB 102 reduction (net				
of SB 633)	—	− 19.6		
Less SB 633 costs	—	− 50.0		
Total, counties	1,888.6	2,026.4	137.8	7.3
Special districts				
Property tax from schools	245.3	273.5		
Total, special districts	245.3	273.5	28.2	11.5
Total	2,411.9	2,457.7	45.8	1.9

Source: State of California, Legislative Analyst, *Summary of Legislative Action on the Budget Bill, 1981–82 Fiscal Year,* (Sacramento: Legislative Analyst, 1981).

Table 4-8
K-12 Schools and Community Colleges in the FY 1980-1981 and FY 1981-1982 Budgets
(millions of dollars)

	1980–1981	1981–1982	Percentage Change
K-12 Schools			
Revenue limits	7,252	8,505.3	
State Teachers' Retirement System	168	189.3	
Categoricals and others	1,234	1,565	
Shift in unsecured property-tax roll	—	379	
Total K-12	8,654	9,638.6	11.4
County Superintendents	361	197.2	− 45.4

Table 4–8 continued

	1980–1981	*1981–1982*	*Percentage Change*
Community Colleges			
State	1,091.3	1,082.7	−0.7
Local	339.6	438.6	29.2
Total	1,430.9	1,521.3	6.3
Total K–14 education	10,445.9	11,347.1	8.6
Less local share	3,395.5	3,990.5	17.5
Total, state share	7,050.4	7,356.6	4.3

Sources: Calculated from: State of California, Legislative Analyst, *Analysis of the Budget Bill FY 1981–82* (Sacramento: Legislative Analyst, 1981); and State of California, Legislative Analyst, *Summary of Legislative Action of the Budget Bill, 1981–82 Fiscal Year* (Sacramento: Legislative Analyst, 1981).

In summary, at the completion of the three cycles of response to Proposition 13, policymaking processes at the state level had largely returned to normal patterns. The financing of education and of the health-and-welfare buy-outs were virtually line items in the state budget. Revenue growth at the local-government level was treated as substantially equivalent to revenue growth at the state level, available for allocation via the state budget. The political ramifications of this transformation of the California intergovernmental fiscal system are considered in chapter 5. The fiscal situation of California state and local governments three years after passage of Proposition 13, and the limited information on the measure's impacts on services and policymaking will now be examined.

California Local and State Governments after Proposition 13

Whereas table 4–8 accurately represents the total revenues available for local education in FY 1981–1982 (barring supplementary appropriations from the state), table 4–7 does not represent total revenues available to cities, counties, and special districts. All three types of local governments have other sources of revenues and none are subject to the revenue limits imposed on schools in 1972 (SB 90), so they may seek to increase their revenues. Although all are subject to the limits imposed by Proposition 4 in 1979, no jursidiction is known to have come close to that limit. Nor, parenthetically, has the state come close; the Legislative Analyst estimated that the governor's proposed FY 1981–1982 budget was $1.1 billion below the limit (1981a).

As noted in the analysis of the deliberations on the first bail-out after Proposition 13, good information on the revenues and expenditures of special districts, cities, and counties was not available in 1978. This situation persisted, and the inadequacy of the normal data source, the State Controller's annual compilation of self-reported data from local governments, has stimulated the commission of special analyses intended to obtain improved data.

The results of a late-1979 survey of selected types of special districts conducted by the State Auditor General are shown in table 4-9. Substantial effects are seen. Many nonenterprise special districts were hard hit by the reductions of property taxes under Proposition 13, and despite the provision of fiscal assistance annually since 1978, some remain substantially affected by the loss of property-tax revenues and the inability to increase alternative revenues. Those strategies have worked better for enterprise districts. As an example, the State of California Auditor General (1980, p. 49) reports:

> Although a substantial percentage of nonenterprise districts reported that they have increased or have instituted fees and charges, the revenue generated from these sources was relatively small when compared to the revenue generated by enterprise districts. For example, the nonenterprise Hayward Area Recreation and Park District in Alameda County, serving a population exceeding 200,000, increased existing fees and charges and instituted new fees and charges in fiscal year 1978-1979. The district generated an additional $73,603 from fees and charges in fiscal year 1978-79. This amount equals about two percent of the $3,726,723 property tax revenue reduction that Hayward Area Recreation and Park District experienced in fiscal year 1978-79. In contrast, the enterprise Tuolumne County Water District No. 2, which provides sewage service to 2,000 customers and water service to 1,100 customers, recovered an additional $120,000 by raising user charges in fiscal year 1978-79, a recovery of 95 percent of the $126,000 property tax revenue it lost in fiscal year 1978-79. Thus, the enterprise district was able to recover a significantly large proportion of its property tax revenue reduction by raising its fees and charges.

More recent data are available for city and county governments in an analysis of the changes in their fiscal conditions between FY 1977-1978 and FY 1979-1980 prepared by Kevin Bacon of the Assembly Office of Research (1981). Table 4-10 reports the summary data for cities and table 4-11 for counties. Twenty-three percent of California cities (65 percent of the 150 cities surveyed) and 31 percent of California counties (86 percent of the 21 counties surveyed) provided full responses to the survey on which these analyses are based. Despite the relatively small proportion of jurisdictions for which data were received, the analysis is believed to be representative, based on the generally good coverage of all sizes of jurisdictions, all regions

Table 4–9
Responses of Special Districts to Proposition 13, FY 1978–1979

District Type	Number of Districts	Number Responding To Survey	Percentage Increasing or Establishing Fees, Charges or Assessments	Percentage Changes in Personnel	Percentage Reducing Operations	Percentage Reducing Capital Outlays	Percentage Studying Organization Changes
Nonenterprise							
Fire protection	454	225	11.1	−1.7	42.2	61.8	36.9
Recreation and parks	118	71	80.3	−30.0	78.9	74.6	22.5
Reclamation	157	69	27.5	−5.7	13.0	14.5	8.7
Flood control	35	20	50.0	−19.1	60.0	55.0	30.0
Enterprise							
County water	205	79	55.7	−0.2	21.5	30.4	25.3
California water	163	35	54.3	11.4	11.4	14.3	22.9
Irrigation	102	60	50.0	0.6	10.0	20.0	31.7
Municipal water	47	33	57.6	1.8	36.4	54.5	27.3

Source: State of California, Office of the Auditor General, *Special Districts: Opportunities for Benefits Through Jurisdictional Changes* (Sacramento: Joint Legislative Audit Committee, California Legislature, 1980).

Table 4-10
Changes in City Finances, FY 1977-1978 to FY 1979-1980 (excluding San Francisco)
(dollars)

	1977–1978	1979–1980	Percentage Change
Revenue trends			
Total city revenues	5.25 billion	5.78 billion	10.1
Total city revenues per capita	326	342	4.9
Total city revenues per capita in constant 1977–1978 dollars	326	299	−8.2
Per capita city discretionary revenues	211	232	9.8
Per-capita city discretionary revenues in constant 1977–1978 dollars	211	202	−4.3
Expenditure trends[a]			
Police and fire	113	114	0.8
Public works	57	50	−12.3
Libraries	8	7	−12.5
Parks and recreation	25	23	−8.0
Other programs	41	35	−14.6
General government	45	37	−17.8
Total (excludes capital outlays)	289	266	−7.8

	Percentage Change 1977–1978 to 1979–1980
Employment trends	
Total city employment in sample cities (nonenterprise-fund activities)	−8.1
Total city employment in all California cities (includes enterprise-fund activities)	−2.1

Source: Kevin R. Bacon, *City and County Finances in the Post-Proposition 13 Era* (Sacramento: Assembly Office of Research, 1981).

[a]City expenditures per capita in constant 1977–1978 dollars.

of the state, and general agreement of response data with other sources. The authors of the report caution that the smallest cities and counties (under 10,000 population) are underrepresented.

While total city and county revenues increased over the study period (from the base year of FY 1977–1978 prior to Proposition 13 to FY 1979–1980 two budget cycles later) when measured in per-capita constant dollars, revenue declines of 8.2 percent occurred in cities and 7.4 percent in counties. The tables also show changes by expenditure category and in employment trends. Police and fire expenditures (shown as "public protection" for

Table 4-11

Changes in County Finances, FY 1977-1978 to FY 1979-1980 (including San Francisco)

(dollars)

	1977-1978	1979-1980	Percentage Change
Revenue trends (58 counties)[a]			
Adjusted total revenues	8.68 billion	9.51 billion	9.5
Adjusted total revenues per capita	389	410	5.4
Adjusted total revenues per capita in constant 1977-1978 dollars	389	360	-7.4
Per-capita county discretionary revenues	153	154	0.6
Per-capita county discretionary revenues in constant 1977-1978 dollars	153	134	-12.4
Expenditure trends[b] (18 counties)[c]			
General government	50	40	-20.0
Public protection	84	88	4.8
Roads	15	16	4.8
Health and sanitation	74	70	-5.9
Public assistance	163	132	-18.9
Libraries and education	5	4	-18.9
Recreation and cultural	7	6	-20.3
Debt service	2	2	-14.3
Total	401	358	-10.7

	Percentage Change 1977-1978 to 1979-1980
Employment trends	
Total county employment in sample counties (includes hospital enterprises)	-2.4

Source: Kevin R. Bacon, *City and County Finances in a Post-Proposition Era* (Sacramento: Assembly Office of Research, 1981).

[a]All county revenue figures have been adjusted to reflect state assumption of county Medi-Cal and SSI/SSP costs.

[b]The expenditure data shown above is based on 18 survey counties, including most of the largest counties. Spending figures shown above are slightly larger than the averages for all 58 counties but the changes are representative of the trends in all counties.

[c]County expenditures per capita are in constant 1977-1978 dollars.

counties) were clearly preserved; other expenditures fell, as did employment. Counties were less able to expand discretionary revenues (those revenues whose expenditure they could decide without federal or state control) than were cities, and both had reduced capacity to respond to local needs.

Table 4-12
Tax and Nontax Revenue Support of City and County Budgets, FY 1977-1978 and FY 1979-1980
(percentages)

	Cities		Counties	
	Percentages of Revenues		*Percentages of Revenues*	
Type of Revenue	*1977-1978*	*1979-1980*	*1977-1978*	*1979-1980*
Tax-based revenues				
Property, sales, and local taxes	49.1	45.4	40.0	26.4
State-shared taxes	7.2	8.0	5.3	6.0
Federal revenue sharing	3.8	3.7	3.4	3.4
Federal and state grants	19.5	16.5	34.9	42.3
Total	79.6	73.6	83.6	78.1
Nontax revenues				
Hospital charges	—	—	7.4	8.8
Other user charges	7.8	9.9	4.2	5.4
Licenses, permits, fines	3.8	4.0	1.9	2.2
Other revenues	8.8	12.5	2.9	5.5
Total	20.4	26.4	16.4	21.9

Source: Compiled from Kevin R. Bacon, *City and County Finances in the Post-Proposition 13 Era* (Sacramento: Assembly Office of Research, 1981).

Table 4-12 reports changes in the sources of city and county revenues over the study period. Tax-based revenues declined in both types of jurisdictions; each received about 5 percent less of their total revenues from taxes in 1979-1980 than in 1977-1978. As would be suggested by the previous analysis of the pattern of state fiscal assistance, federal and state grants increased for counties and decreased for cities: while such grants increased 15.9 percent for counties, they declined 11.5 percent for cities.

Larger cities and larger counties have both been affected more by Proposition 13 than have smaller jurisdictions. For example, in the five cities with populations greater than 300,000 responding to the Assembly Office of Research survey, total revenues expanded by only 7.9 percent between 1977-1978 and 1979-1980, compared with an average of 11.5 percent for five categories of smaller cities (10.1 percent for all cities). The five responding counties with populations greater than 1 million experienced revenue growth of 7.3 percent, compared with 13.3 percent for four categories of smaller counties (9.5 percent for all counties). Los Angeles and Oakland, two of the largest cities in the study, had particular difficulty in adjusting to Proposition 13. Both lost disproportionate amounts of revenue because they had high property taxes, and both carried the burden of generous city pension systems that diverted revenues from current uses. Their reductions in programs and staffs exceeded the average in other cities, although it must be noted that their revenues before Proposition 13 were relatively high. In FY 1977–1978 Los Angeles had total revenues of $428 and Oakland $473 per resident, compared with a statewide average of $346 of city revenues per capita (State of California, State Controller 1978). Both jurisdictions attempted to impose additional special taxes under the provisions provided in Proposition 13, but the electorates of both cities rejected the appeals, even when the new tax revenues were to go to police services.

The Assembly Office of Research study (Bacon 1981) also provided information on service levels, data that are rarely available for a cross section of local jurisdictions. The summary conclusions concerning cities and counties are:

City Service Levels

In response to Proposition 13's major cut in city tax revenues, most cities were forced to trim local services. Generally speaking, fire and police services were spared from serious cutbacks. Virtually every community we visited indicated that the local city council put fire and police services at the top of their priority list. As a result of sparing this large sector of the city budget (40 percent in most cities) heavier cuts fell on the remaining areas. The areas most frequently affected were library operations, park and recreation programs, street maintenance programs, general city administrative offices, and a variety of city supplied social and community services.

Our survey indicates that cities have been able to maintain police and fire department response times during the study period in the face of rising demand for these services. Cities have not, however, been able to hold constant the average ratio of sworn police officers per 10,000 residents (dropping 7.2 percent from 16.7 to 15.5 officers per 10,000 residents) or firemen per 10,000 residents (dropping 6.4 percent from 17.1 to 16.0 firemen per 10,000 residents). This decline could indicate that cities may not be able to maintain the current level of fire and police service in future years.

City street maintenance programs suffered significant cutbacks during the study period. While the total street mileage in our survey cities rose by 3.1 percent, the number of miles repaved or treated with a major maintenance treatment dropped 6.7 percent. Several large cities (Los Angeles, Oakland) now have stretched their maintenance cycles to the extent that their street systems are guaranteed to deteriorate. Though many city officials express dissatisfaction with the practice, street maintenance programs are viewed as an "invisible" place to cut spending in the short run.

Park and library programs showed the largest declines in the level of public service. In our sample, libraries have reduced public service hours by an average of 14.7 percent over the study period. They have also trimmed spending on books by 15.4 percent after adjustment has been made for the effects of inflation. Park and recreation program staff have been cut by an average 15.6 percent over this period and cuts in park maintenance workers have resulted in 19.7 percent increase in the acreage of park land maintained by each worker.

County Service Levels

Our survey results indicate that the level of police protection services has slipped somewhat over the study period. Sheriff's department response times have slowed about 10 percent in the ten counties supplying this information on our survey (response time increased by an average of 1 minute in our sample). While the total number of sworn and civilian law enforcement employees increased in our survey counties, the *ratio* of sworn officers per 10,000 residents fell from 7.1 to 6.9 (− 2.8 percent) during the study period. If this trend continues counties will experience a further decline in service in this area. In general, while county law enforcement budgets have kept pace with inflation, they have not been able to increase staffing in proportion to growth in population and rising crime rates.

In general, county road programs reflected a decline similar to that shown by city programs. There was a 9.5 percent decline in the number of miles of road repaved or treated with a major maintenance procedure over the study period. Counties in our survey reported widely varying changes in this area. Sharp decreases were reported by Yolo (− 25 percent), Riverside (− 42 percent), and Los Angeles (− 12 percent), while large increases were reported by Alameda (13 percent) and Orange (43 percent).

As was the case with cities, county library and park programs made sharp cutbacks in public services. Library public service hours declined by 19.4 percent, the number of branch libraries fell by 10 percent, and library book purchases (inflation adjusted) fell by 12 percent. County parks and recreation programs were forced to reduce staff by nearly 48 percent and to increase the workload of maintenance staff by increasing the acreage of park land maintained by each worker 26 percent.

Local governments responded to their new fiscal condition not only by cutting budgets and services and increasing revenues where possible but also by pursuing innovations intended to provide services at lower costs. If data series on revenues and expenditures are inadequate, those on changes made to improve productivity are nonexistent. One survey of city actions in this regard was undertaken by the League of California Cities, with grant support from the Intergovernmental Personnel Act, United States Office of Personnel, as part of an Innovation Exchange Program intended to share innovative ideas among cities (League of California Cities 1980). The League reported innovations by jurisdiction. A total of 422 jurisdictions undertook innovations in response to Proposition 13. A number of cities, all small or middle-size, initiated several innovations.

The League named seven areas of innovation demonstrating the greatest potential for cost reduction without serious disruption. Their discussion of these areas gives an idea of the ferment involved (League of California Cities 1980):

Para-Professionals in Public Safety

Use of paraprofessionals in public safety is a cost-cutting technique utilized by the cities of Irvine (65,000 pop.), Fairfield (54,391 pop.), Modesto (102,272 pop.), and Stockton (127,285 pop.). The para-professionals are civilian public safety employees who respond to calls and perform duties that do not require sworn police or fire personnel. Typical duties of civilian personnel include report writing, records management, dispatch, some traffic investigations, issuing traffic citations, assisting in crowd and traffic control at fires, and other related functions.

The cities using this approach report a number of positive results. They have increased the number of personnel to meet the needs of their growing communities while realizing cost savings by hiring civilians whose salaries and fringe benefits are less than regular public safety employees. Paraprofessional programs also provide a career ladder for civilian employees, and some have gone on to become regular sworn officers.

Increasing Productivity in the Budget Process

Another innovation which may see more widespread use throughout the state was developed by the City of Fairfield (54,391 pop.) and recently modified by Morro Bay (9,000 pop.) to use fewer staff resources in the budget process. Fairfield's two page budget for general fund expenditures and Morro Bay's five page program budget are the result of a public attitude that allows changes in local government without delays caused by extensive time consuming studies.

Instead of taking up large amounts of city council and staff time poring over budget details, decision making at the top is limited to setting overall spending limits for each city department. Fairfield's budget document adopted for two fiscal years allows departments to carry 80% of any surplus foward to the following year's budget. The system makes a bottom line allocation, without separate personnel or capital outlay allocations, to the following departments: Public Works, Public Safety, Environmental Affairs, Finance, Recreation, City Attorney, Data Processing and Administration. The base year budget was the City's Proposition 13 budget without the state bail-out funds. Expenditures are allowed to increase based on a formula which uses San Francisco Bay Area cost of living index and growth in Fairfield's housing units.

Fairfield estimates an annual savings of over 1,000 person-hours and $40,000 by not performing the normal budget process. Carryover of unexpended funds have increased from 3.9% to 8.1%. This carryover was from a budget more than 5% below what the figure would have been under the old conventional budget process. The formula used to increase the budget tells department heads what this dollar appropriation will be from year to year so they can plan their expenditures accordingly.

Local Government Marketing Techniques

Few municipal programs were hit as hard by the "taxpayer revolt" as city parks and recreation. Some cities are now using marketing techniques to encourage private donations of time and money to keep their park and recreation programs and facilities operating.

The City of Pasadena (108,000 pop.) has created a Recreation and Parks Foundation to sponsor a "Parks Need Friends Too" program. Individuals, companies, school classes, church groups and service clubs are encouraged to make tax deductible donations which can be earmarked to provide specific items such as benches, picnic tables, slides, trees, or buildings at a designated park. Contributors are recognized by a certificate, plaque, or more elaborate memorial, depending on the amount and item donated.

In Ventura (70,000 pop.), the city has developed a "Gifts Book for Parks and Recreation" catalog. The catalog lists items which contributors may wish to support. Donations from individuals, groups or the business community can be designated for items ranging from playground equipment to recreation programs, activities and events.

Consolidation/Reorganization of Local Government

Consolidation or reorganization of local government services have also grown more popular among California cities. The cities of Corte Madera (8,647 pop.) and Larkspur (12,375 pop.) have shared the services of one police chief since January, 1979. The arrangement was initially offered to Larkspur by Corte Madera for a three month period while Larkspur went through the recruitment process to fill their police chief vacancy. It became apparent that sharing was not causing any problems; instead, duplication of effort was reduced or eliminated while better and broader service was delivered at less expense.

After sixty days of sharing a police chief, the two city managers reported to their councils and received approval to work for six months on making the arrangement permanent. It worked so well that the cities decided to go even further. On July 1, 1980, the cities of Corte Madera and Larkspur consolidated the two police departments, with a formal Joint Powers Agreement establishing the Twin Cities Police Department, directed by the Twin Cities Police Council.

Positive results of consolidation include uniformity of police procedures, less duplication of effort, better coordination in areas such as investigations and work with juveniles, and an improved level of service at less cost. The consolidation also presented an opportunity to improve the department's organizational structure.

Another example of a consolidation of services is the joint delivery of fire protection services by San Carlos (26,236 pop.) and Belmont (25,909 pop.). In the early 1970's, the Belmont Fire District became a subsidiary district of the City of Belmont. Since that time, the Belmont city council has acted as the fire district's Board of Directors.

In 1977, prior to the passage of Proposition 13, the Belmont Fire District approached the City of San Carlos, proposing a feasibility study on the consolidation of the two fire departments. A short feasibility study was developed and submitted to the two agencies. The study recommended a more extensive report be prepared.

Proposition 13 was approved while the consolidation study was being conducted. The consolidation effort gained momentum when the initiative forced each city to eliminate a fire station. In addition, San Carlos had already signed Joint Powers Agreements with other agencies for civil defense, wastewater treatment, and other services.

Both elected and appointed officials were involved in the consolidation of the two fire departments into the South County Fire Protection Authority. The Policy Liaison Committee, established by the two city councils and consisting of the mayor and vice-mayor from each city, was instrumental in handling the political and public concerns about the consolidation. The committee addressed policy issues while allowing staff to work out administrative details.

The Belmont Fire District and San Carlos Fire Department administrative staffs were consolidated on July 1, 1979. The consolidation affected the Chief, battalion chiefs, fire marshall, and staff. Captains and firefighters remained under their respective jurisdictions.

On January 1, 1980, both fire departments were completely merged into the South County Fire Protection Authority. The Board of Directors consists of two council members from each city. Costs are shared on a 50/50 basis with San Carlos providing office space and dispatch. Belmont provides finance, personnel and garage services.

Consolidation has improved protection for each of the communities. After Proposition 13, each city operated two fire stations and two engine companies. South County Fire now operates four fire stations and four engine companies, but it also operates a ladder company and a rescue unit. Also, two fire prevention inspectors have beed added to improve service.

Other positive results include savings realized by the elimination of a fire chief, a fire marshall, three battalion chief positions and the standardization of the fire codes for each of the cities.

Contracting for Local Government Services

Contracting out for local government services is one of the most common cutback strategies being used by California cities. In Corcoran (5,775 pop.), an interesting arrangement has been developed by the city and the local YMCA. Prior to the passage of Proposition 13, the City of Corcoran employed 64 persons. The city currently has 38 employees. To continue city services despite the cutback in personnel, Corcoran has contracted with the local YMCA for all recreation services since September 1, 1977. Length of the contract is 4 years, 10 months.

Corcoran also contracted with the YMCA for maintenance of the community park at a cost of $24,600 per year. This arrangement continued until August 7, 1978, when Corcoran deeded its community center and the community park to the YMCA with the stipulation that the YMCA continue to provide recreation services for the city. Corcoran retains two neighborhood parks in addition to the community park deeded to the YMCA.

This arrangement has cut the city's costs and has prevented a duplication of recreation services by the two agencies. According to the city, the contract system allows the YMCA to provide more recreation services than the two agencies could have provided separately.

The local YMCA director feels the agency is better able to obtain donations and is more successful at getting volunteers than the city would be. For example, the YMCA's recreational facilities are financed primarily by the Corcoran Foundation, which receives the majority of its funds from the Boswell Foundation.

Joint Ventures in Local Government

One of the more popular innovations adopted by California's cities has been municipal self insurance pools. A League survey conducted in January found there are currently 13 municipal self insurance groups operating in California providing insurance coverage for 128 cities, 2 counties, and a school district. Participant coverage includes Workers' Compensation with some members also self insured for General Liability and Employee Medical and Dental Benefits.

Public/Private Partnerships

Public/private partnerships are being utilized more by cities to maintain service levels. For example, the City of El Segundo (15,750 pop.) is home for several major industrial and aerospace manufacturing plants. These plants typically operate around the clock, seven days a week, and are constantly engaged in repairing or altering buildings and facilities at their vast plant sites.

To reduce the burden on the city's building inspectors and to expedite the inspection of numerous small construction projects at these major industries, the city created the Deputy Inspector Program ten years ago. Deputy Inspectors are employees of these major industries and are authorized, for an annual $100 fee, to inspect on behalf of the city small and moderate sized construction projects performed by contractors and sub-contractors at their El Segundo plants. The Deputy Inspectors, like Building Inspectors, must pass an examination testing their knowledge of the building, electrical, or plumbing codes. They may inspect construction, maintenance, and repair projects not exceeding one story or 2,500 square feet and which require no engineering work. They may not inspect work performed by fellow company employees unless specifically authorized to do so by the city's building official. All the work performed is subject to the customary permits and fees and they are expected to submit quarterly reports. Penalty provisions are included in the ordinance creating this program and a Deputy Inspector's authorization can be revoked.

Seven major industries have taken advantage of the program, and eleven individuals have been authorized to inspect construction work, nine authorized to inspect electrical work, and one authorized to inspect plumbing work. Although there was some initial concern that company employees would be lax and uncritical in their inspections, this has not been the case. The Deputy Inspector program has worked well, saving both industries and the city time and money. The frustrating delays the industries used to complain about are no longer a problem. The city estimates at least five additional full-time inspectors would have to be hired to do the work currently performed by the Deputy Inspectors. In addition, the program has improved relations between these major industrial residents and the city government.

Among the other cost cutting ideas being implemented by California cities are joint ventures for the recruitment and testing of employees, joint

powers authorities for programming and data processing, volunteer programs utilizing citizens to supplement the municipal work force, and limited term contracts with public safety personnel.

Even this listing of innovations does not do full justice to the responses of
cities to Proposition 13. In addition to service provision, cities and counties
also engaged in a variety of licensing and regulatory activities (such as local
ordinances and business licenses), of which the most important was land-
use regulation. Land-use regulation in California is complex, operating
within a state-developed legal context that can only be described as convo-
luted, time-consuming, and biased against development (Kirlin 1981a). Four
types of policy changes in land-use policymaking by local governments can
be traced at least in considerable part to Proposition 13. An early and visible
response was a substantial increase in the fees associated with development
(Chapman 1981). Given reduced property-tax revenues from new development and general fiscal stress, some local jurisdictions also hesitated to
allow new development, or at least scrutinized its cost-and-revenue implications more closely (State of California, Office of Planning and Research
1979, 1980). Three policy initiatives were launched, each advocated by some
state agencies but implemented locally, to provide access to housing for
those of low and moderate income. These initiatives arose partly in response
to Proposition 13, but more in response to the overall restriction on the production of housing in California that was the legacy of public policies that
increased housing prices from the national average in 1974 to 50 percent
above that figure from 1977 on. The three initiatives were rent control, bans
or tight regulations on condominium conversions, and inclusionary zoning,
each of which further exacerbated the problem by constraining housing production (Kirlin 1981a). Finally, a few jurisdictions began to use their powers
of land-use regulation imaginatively, achieving their plans for development
within their boundaries while obtaining desired developer-financed public
improvements, or even participating in developers' profits from commercial
projects so that nontax revenues flowed to the cities (Kirlin and Chapman
1980).

　　To complete analysis of the impact of Propostion 13 on the intergovernmental fiscal system of California, attention must return to state government. The earlier analysis of the state budget emphasized the provision of
fiscal assistance to local governments. Now that the fiscal situation of local
governments has been examined, albeit in varying levels of detail as dictated
by available data, what can be said of the state's fiscal situation in FY
1981–1982, four budget-years after Proposition 13?

　　Table 4–13 analyzes the fiscal condition of the state, as measured by
general-fund revenues and expenditures and total state employees for FY
1977–1978 and FY 1981–1982 (budgeted). In constant per-capita terms,
revenues were up 2.0 percent, and increases in state-government employ-

Table 4-13
Changes in the State of California General-Fund Revenues and
Expenditures
(millions of dollars)

	1977-1978	1981-1982 (Budgeted)	Percentage Change
Revenues			
Total general fund	13,695	21,020	53.5
Per capita, constant dollars	370	377	2.0
Expenditures			
Direct state outlays	3,185	4,568	43.5
Per capita, constant dollars	86	82	−4.7
Assistance to local governments	8,500	17,104	101.2
Per capita, constant dollars	229	307	33.7
State employment			
Total	221,251	225,984	2.1
Per capita	.0100	.0096	−4.0

Sources: Calculated from State of California, Legislative Analyst, *Analysis of the Budget Bill, 1981–82* (Sacramento: Legislative Analyst, 1981); and Legislative Analyst, *Summary of Legislative Action on the Budget Bill, 1981–82* (Sacramento: Legislative Analyst, 1981).

ment were up 2.1 percent. The composition of general-fund expenditures shifted; state operations increased 43.5 percent while state assistance to local governments (including the Proposition-13-induced fiscal relief) increased by just over 100 percent. As a consequence, the proportion of general-fund expenditures going to state operations declined from 27 percent to 21 percent. In comparison with cities and counties, the state fared relatively well in the wake of Jarvis-Gann. Total revenues increased in real per-capita terms, and because of the availability of the surplus the state was able to provide substantially increased assistance to local governments while very slightly increasing state employment. In deflated per-capita terms, direct state outlays declined 4.7 percent over four budget cycles, roughly half the decline that cities and counties experienced over two budget cycles. Moreover, as the Legislative Analyst argues, nearly $7 billion of what is termed "local assistance" in the budget was really assistance to individuals, the conditions and funding of which the state controlled, but the payments of which were made by local government (for example, $2.6 billion in county-provided medical assistance to low-income individuals, or $1.2 billion in state-funded AFDC benefits)(Legislative Analyst 1981a). The next chapter will further explore the political dynamics that yielded this pattern of state policymaking.

5 Restructuring the California Political System

The analysis of the roots of Proposition 13 and the general Fiscal Limits Movement undertaken in the first three chapters of this volume emphasized their political causes in addition to the more commonly discussed economic factors. Just as important causes of this phenomenon were political, so too were its effects political. Chapter 4 examined the fiscal consequences of Proposition 13 and related developments. This chapter seeks to both provide further explanation of certain responses to Proposition 13 and to examine the impact of Propositions 13 and 4 and the policies developed in response to them on the political system of California.

First, the political impact of a sharp fiscal constraint on the size of the public sector is examined. Second, the spillover effects of this issue on elections to public office and on the initiative process are analyzed in light of the expectation that an event of this magnitude might have influence on the election chances of candidates and stimulate more initiatives. Third, the impact of fiscal constraint on the intergovernmental system, that is, on the relationships among the state and local governments, is studied. Fourth, the possibility that Proposition 13 advanced some policy issues on the political agenda and repressed others is considered. Fifth, the dynamics of the process by which the state legislature became more ascendant in policymaking are analyzed.

Redefining the Size of the California Public Sector

The first, and initially very powerful, political impact of Proposition 13 was to shrink the size of the California public sector. California dropped from among the highest-taxing states in the nation to near middle rank and, in per-capita constant dollars, expenditures fell for California state, city, and county governments. Proposition 13 and subsequent, related actions imposed a real fiscal constraint on California governments, which resulted in several consequences.

Probably the most powerful consequence was the challenge posed to previously dominant ideas as to what constituted a good public sector. This definition, especially in California, commonly emphasized the function of government in providing services and in balancing interest groups (with a special obligation to the disadvantaged), and in pursuing social good through an expanded and (almost always) more-expensive public sector. The clearest evidence of this orientation was seen in the analysis of tax-reform deliberations in the California legislature in the decade before passage of the Jarvis-Gann Initiative.

It could be argued that those California public officials and interest groups who supported continued expansion of public-sector revenues before 1978 were Pollyannaish; that such a trend could not long continue. Perhaps so, but this argument misses the more important point that they positively valued such an expansion, believing fervently in government that used its powers, and particularly the power of the public purse, to redress perceived social problems. Primary among these perceived social problems was unequal distribution of income and wealth, and the California legislature sought assiduously to direct both taxes and expenditures to benefit the poor in the decade before Proposition 13.

To identify these values and to analyze the policies they stimulated is not to judge their appropriateness. They existed and were powerful influences on policymaking. After Proposition 13, most California public officials appeared to hold to the same objective of improving the public good through public policy, and were still committed to aiding the disadvantaged. Though the winds of electoral change resulted in a modest increase in more-conservative legislators, most post-Proposition 13 members of the California legislature, and all of those holding leadership positions, were in that body before passage of Proposition 13. Most of the senior analytic staff of the legislature were also veterans of the era before fiscal limits, as was Governor Brown.

It was not the goals that changed but the wherewithal to achieve them. There was, simply put, less money in the public sector. In this regard, the consequences of Proposition 13 accord well with what Clark and Ferguson (1981) argued was an emerging tendency among the populace to be liberal in policy but fiscally conservative.

For the state, fiscal constraint occurred not only because it provided relief to local governments, but also because it indexed personal-income taxes, which the Legislative Analyst estimated would reduce state revenues by $2.7 billion in FY 1981–1982 and $3.5 billion in FY 1982–1983 (1981). However, the Legislative Analyst also estimated that after FY 1982–1983, when indexing would again be limited to the rate of inflation above 3 percent, personal-income tax revenues would probably grow an average of 10 to 20 percent faster than personal income (1981a). This implied an elasticity ratio of taxes to personal income of about 1.15, compared with the estimate of 1.65 before Proposition 13 (see table 3–3). Combined with increasing revenues from other positively elastic sources of revenue (sales taxes should maintain their prior elasticity ratio of 1.15), state revenues could begin to rise again. Eventually, the Proposition-4 limit could constrain this revenue growth, but in the absence of public pressure to rebate any excess revenues, the legislature would probably find a way to circumvent that limit.

Ultimately, the constraints on state revenues were political and perceptual, and those imposed by the performance of the economy not statutory nor even constitutional. While the voters rejected Proposition 9, and the initiative to abolish the sales tax failed to qualify, the behavior of state legislators suggested that they hesitated to impose any new taxes or to overtly increase existing taxes. Although willing to exploit loopholes in the Gann Initiative, or to let full indexing of the personal-income tax expire under an existing sunset provision, legislators were hesitant to increase the state tax on gasoline, despite the fact that inflation had greatly eroded real yield and gas-tax revenues were badly needed for state road maintenance, not to mention new construction. Local governments, which shared in gasoline-tax revenues collected by the state, were even more in need of additional revenues for road maintenance. As an extreme but not singular example, the city of Oakland shifted from a 30-year to a 100-year cycle for street resurfacing, virtually ensuring the destruction of its streets. An increase in the gasoline tax was passed in 1981.

One indication of the electorate's sentiment toward additional taxes was seen in their vote to impose a "special tax," as allowed by Proposition 13, a tax requiring a two-thirds majority for passage. Twenty-eight cities placed special taxes on the ballot, and nine (32 percent) were approved. In 1979, a statute was enacted that allowed two mechanisms for raising revenues for fire and police services. One was comparable to a benefit-assessment district and the second to a special tax. Each required a two-thirds majority for approval. Thirteen cities placed such measures before the voters; five (38 percent) were approved.

In sum, California public-sector revenues were reduced by the passage of Proposition 13 and related events, a reduction that at least reduced the state's public sector on a one-time basis. Moreover, the evidence available to date suggests that although future revenue growth may modestly exceed the growth in personal income of California residents, no major increases in revenues are likely. The values and policy objectives of California public officials do not appear to be substantially different than those prior to June, 1978, but the fiscal resources to pursue those objectives are more limited.

The Impact of Fiscal Limits on Electoral Processes

Conflict in elections, reflecting patterns of conflict in society, is usually cyclical. The 1950s, for example, were a period of relative quiet in national politics. More conflict was evident in the mid- and late 1960s, focused on civil rights, environmental issues, and the Vietnam War. The early 1970s held less conflict; in the later 1970s the tax revolt spread. Over a decade ago, Coleman (1957) presented an elegant examination of why conflict in communities is episodic; evidence to this effect has been provided by others (Agger et al. 1964; Kammerer et al. 1963; Kirlin 1975). Nie et al. (1976) provide a review of evidence on changing attitudes and electoral behavior of the national electorate that also supports the theory that conflict and change are cyclical. Such a cyclical pattern is one of the attributes of the four-sector political-process model advanced in chapter 1. Thus, prior research and theory-building suggest that the sizable conflict seen in California concerning taxes in 1978 was unlikely to have been confined to a single ballot choice on a single election day.

As mentioned in chapter 4, an unusually large number of incumbent legislators (six members of the Assembly and two of the Senate), all Democrats, were defeated in the November, 1978 general elections, the first elections after passage of Proposition 13. General elections were held again in November, 1980, with all Assembly seats and half of the Senate seats up for election. Of the six Republican "Proposition-13 babies" in the Assembly, who had defeated incumbent Democrats with the aid of computerized "personal" letters to voters from Howard Jarvis, only one (Hayes) was defeated in the 1980 campaign. The two similarly situated senators were not up for election until 1982. During the 1977–1978 session, immediately preceding passage of Jarvis-Gann, the Assembly contained fifty-six Democrats and twenty-four Republicans; after the November, 1980 election, the lineup included forty-seven Democrats and thirty-three Republicans. In the Senate, representation in the 1977–1978 session consisted of twenty-six Democrats and fourteen Republicans. After the 1980 election twenty-three Democrats and seventeen Republicans sat in the Senate. Electoral contests for the California legislature have, thus, been modestly affected by a spurt of general political conflict attendant on passage of Proposition 13. But the change in partisan lineup has not been very dramatic, and Republicans remain the minority party.

Equivalent data for electoral conflict at the local level are not available in any systematic data series. Of course, California local elections are nonpartisan, so the relevant measure would be turnover among incumbent officeholders. There is some evidence that turnover has increased. Two incumbent supervisors of Los Angeles County were defeated by more-conservative challengers in 1980, extraordinarily rare events historically. Moreover, one analysis of local recall elections found that they had increased dramatically, from approximately ten annually in 1973 to forty-five late in 1979 (Quinn 1979).

More substantial support for the episodic-conflict theory can be found in the pattern of activity concerning initiatives. California is the only large state in which the initiative process (adopted in 1911) can be used to adopt both statutes and constitutional provisions. From 1912 through mid–1980, 473 initiatives were circulated in the state. Of these, 167 qualified to be placed on the ballot, receiving 5 percent of the total number of votes for governor in the last election in the case of statutory initiatives and 8 percent in the case of constitutional initiatives; 45 were adopted (State of California, Secretary of State 1979; Fitzgerald 1980). Prior to passage of Proposition 13, only 1 of nearly 100 proposed initiatives dealing with taxation had been adopted (abolition of the poll tax in 1914).

Initiative activity tripled after 1970. Prior to 1970, attempts to qualify initiatives were made 4.7 times per year on the average. Since 1970, an average of 15.3 initiatives per year have been circulated. Fewer initiatives have qualified for the ballot in recent years (15 percent since 1970 versus 55 percent in the prior years). The percentage approved by the electorate had been in the 27- to 30-percent range over the seven decades. Some recent initiative campaigns were very expensive. In the 1976–1978 period, millions of dollars were spent to defeat an anti-smoking initiative, to support an initiative establishing statewide regulations of rent control palatable to apartment owners and investors, and to defeat an initiative to increase taxes on oil companies.

In 1981, Howard Jarvis qualified another initiative, to make indexing of the personal-income tax full and permanent. This initiative will appear on the June, 1982 ballot, so the era of initiative-propelled restructuring of the California fiscal system may not be yet complete.

Of course, by 1980 this California experience was being played out as part of a significant challenge to the orthodoxy of federal policymaking, taxing, and spending. From one perspective, the national Reagan victory and subsequent policy initiatives are part of the cycle of conflict over the size and objectives of the public sector, a conflict of which Proposition 13 was an earlier component. At the national level, the episodic-conflict theory appears quite plausible: half of the states adopted one or another form of fiscal limit, Ronald Reagan was elected president, the Republicans have gained control of the Senate, and the Democratic majority in the House of Representatives is in shambles.

Reordering the Public-Policy Agenda

The Fiscal Limits Movement put some policy issues at an advantage by focusing greater attention on them, and other issues at a disadvantage by detracting attention from them. An example of the former is housing; of the latter, school-financing equalization.

Housing was already a sizable issue in California. A well-publicized leap in prices after 1975 provided clear evidence of a shortage of owner-occupied units. Proposition 13 is credited or blamed by some for sparking a wave of local rent-control initiatives or ordinances in California (for example, in San Francisco, Los Angeles, Santa Monica, Davis, and Berkeley). The organizing cry for the rent-control movement became "homeowners got relief from Proposition 13, renters can get it from rent control." Property owners responded with Proposition 10, but this bid to limit rent control was defeated. Proposition 13 also upset established practices for real-estate development, reducing the property-tax revenues that jurisdictions received from any new development to the point where many questioned whether new development provided sufficient revenues to cover increased expenditures (State of California, Office of Planning and Research 1979). Jurisdictions coped by increasing fees and user charges (Chapman and Kirlin 1980) and by entering into innovative agreements with developers (Kirlin and Chapman 1980). In 1979, the legislature adopted and the governor signed a "$100 Million Dollar Housing Program," including $82 million for a new Rental Housing Construction Program, $7.5 million for a Homeownership Assistance Program, $10 million for an expanded deferred-payment rehabilitation-loan program, and $.5 million for departmental administration.

School-finance equalization was a critical public-policy issue in California in the several years prior to passage of the Jarvis-Gann Initiative because of the *Serrano* v. *Priest* court decision that ruled that inequalities in school-district financing resulting from differences in assessed valuations were unconstitutional. The legislature responded by, in the words of State Superintendent of Education Wilson Riles, "averaging up." Differences in expenditures per average daily attendance (ADA) for 95 percent of the state's children were reduced from about $850 in 1971 to approximately $200 from the average in 1978–1979 (Riles 1979). This was accomplished by placing strict revenue limits on all districts, allowing smaller increases for higher-spending districts, and skewing state aid toward low-spending districts. Although the bail-outs after Proposition 13 continued this remedy, the issue has not attracted the same level of attention as it did before Jarvis-Gann. In part this is because of the substantial progress previously made toward equalization. Finally, of course, "averaging up" was a very expensive strategy for complying with the Serrano decision (it was, for example, one of the reasons used to *justify* accumulation of such a large state surplus before Proposition 13) and state revenues previously in excess were now consumed to provide relief for the property-tax losses caused by the Jarvis-Gann initiative. As an indication of the change in orientation, the legislature added $300,000 to the FY 1981–1982 budget appropriation to the State Department of Education for legal defense of present policy against an expected law suit alleging noncompliance with the Serrano decision.

Other policy issues received more discussion as a consequence of fiscal limits, but did not reach clear resolution. The possibility of cost reductions through nontraditional modes of service delivery, and especially through contracting with private firms, was explored in several jurisdictions, but only very limited movement in this direction occurred. In November, 1979, voters in both the city and county of Los Angeles gave strong support (more than 60 percent) to ballot measures removing provisions in their respective charters that prohibited contracts with private firms. Nearly a year-and-a-half later, the city had not entered into any such contracts and the county into only six (*Los Angeles Times* April 27, 1980; and April 28, 1980). Bacon (1981, p. 31) found that cities included in the study by the Assembly Office of Research increased contract payments by 20 percent between 1977–1978 and 1979–1980, but that contracts accounted for only 2.8 percent of total city operating expenditures.

Other structural changes were considered in various local governments. As an example, the city of Los Angeles and Los Angeles County jointly established a citizens' committee to examine possible consolidation of some functions, and the Napa City Council and Napa County Board of Supervisors met to explore possible combination of some activities or intergovernmental contracts. In a reversal of the usual (but often erroneous) orthodox belief that larger jurisdictions are less costly and provide better services, some consideration was given in 1980–1981 to breaking up the Los Angeles Unified School District, the nation's second largest school district, into smaller districts. But no statewide data have been maintained on any structural changes in functions or activities, so no judgment can be made as to whether such activities became more frequent after passage of Proposition 13. Importantly, moreover, the state has not sought to force structural change through putting conditions on its fiscal assistance, despite Governor Brown's suggestion in the summer of 1978 that reducing the number of local governments would save money, a belief initially echoed by, among others, A. Alan Post, the retired long-time legislative analyst who chaired the governor's Commission on Government Reform. The commission, established on June 23, 1978, to study long-term impacts of Proposition 13 and make recommendations for possible government reforms to ameliorate those impacts, consisted of fourteen leaders from business, local government, the press, unions, and the judiciary. The commission was supported in its work by a very small number of state employees assigned to it and by the efforts of hundreds of individuals (local and state officials, university and college faculty, and citizens) who organized into fifty-two task forces on specific topics. The three task forces that focused on the question of possible government reorganization argued strenuously that there was no evidence in previous experience that any centrally directed governmental restructuring would be desirable, and that restructuring was an ongoing process in any case (see Kirlin 1978), a position finally persuasive to most commission members. Their report recommended a "bottoms-up" examination of possible restructuring without any state direction. Whether because of the position taken by the commission, the strong opposition of local government, or some combination of these and other factors, the state has not sought to force local-government reorganization. Nor, parenthetically, has it undertaken to reorganize its own operations.

Pension reform also received additional attention because of Proposition 13, but again with little clear change in previous patterns. Funds for reducing the unfunded liability of the State Teachers' Retirement System were included in AB 8, the long-term fiscal-assistance plan for local government adopted in 1979. The contribution of generous existing pensions for police and fire employees to the fiscal plight of some jurisdictions such as the cities of Los Angeles and Oakland was recognized. In the November, 1980 elections, voters in Los Angeles City approved a charter amendment reducing pension benefits for individuals hired in the fire and police departments after that date. Voters in San Francisco approved a plan that gave currently employed police and fire fighters incentive to subscribe to a less costly pension system; vesting periods were changed at the same election.

The full impact of Proposition 13 and related events on the public-policy agenda of Califonia governments cannot be captured by these examples. The impact is more pervasive, less obtrusive, yet more powerful than the examples suggest. The *language* of policy processes has changed. Before Proposition 13, the common presumption was that revenues were available for most good and important programs. Now this is no longer presumed. Revenues are constrained, and since all participants in policy processes know this, the socially legitimizing language (Cochran 1980) with which to discuss policy choices is that of constraint, of hard choices, of denial of requests for public expenditures.

A More Interdependent Governmental System

The increased fiscal interdependence of California state and local governments is glaringly obvious in the analysis presented in chapter 4. To reiterate, the share of school-district, county, and nonenterprise special-district revenues received in transfers from the state rose sharply. In making these increased fiscal transfers, the state encountered a new level of competition for alternative uses of its revenues. Fearful of a revenue shortfall, the state legislature enacted a deflator clause that specified the amount its aid to local units would decline if the annual revenue projections underlying each year's budget were not met. Even cities, whose proportion of revenues received from the state fell after Proposition 13, were more fiscally dependent on other units of government because the state annually balanced its budget by shifting not only its fiscal-assistance payments among classes of jurisdictions but also shifted revenue bases with almost-equal ease. The expenditure limits imposed by the Gann Initiative bore on all governments in the state. Moreover, calculations of the limits for individual local jurisdictions and the state were interdependent, depending on fiscal assistance transferred or received.

In the pre-Proposition 13 governmental universe of California, local jurisdictions and the state had essentially stable revenue bases and considerable discretion over expenditure of funds from their own revenues. Local governments vied with one another and with the state for access to revenue sources, but the general rule was that once won, a revenue source was not yielded. Thus, cities and counties received (and still receive) one cent of the state-collected sales tax returned to the jurisdiction of point of sale. Schools, cities, counties, and special districts shared access to property taxes, each operating under somewhat different statutory state strictures as to how it should set rates, but all with the assumption of stability in revenue sources and in the basic structure of taxation. This system was shattered by Proposition 13. How the legislature and localities sought to reestablish equilibrium will be discussed on pages 104–107.

The increased interdependence was more than fiscal. Policy and programatic interdependence were already evident in three areas. In buying out county shares of health and welfare expenditures, the state was essentially assuming fiscal responsibility for services it (and the federal government) already largely directed, but the state stake in policymaking in these areas was now heightened, and state officials should have been more conscious of the cost consequences of both their policies and of any local initiatives. Proposition 4 required state reimbursement of costs mandated on local governments, creating the need for much more accurate cost accounting that could only be achieved through vastly more precise determinations of existing local activities and of state-mandated increments. The state responded both by seeking more data and by exploring ways to reduce its need for detailed cost data. The FY 1981–1982 state budget for education illustrated both trends. It required the Department of Finance to audit the distribution of property-tax revenues to school entities in twenty representative counties and provided $100,000 for the Legislative Analyst to study reorganization of the Los Angeles Unified School District. Yet, in the *Analysis of the Budget Bill* (1981, pp. 1173–1174), the Legislative Analyst proposed that school districts not be required to keep detailed cost records of costs associated with collective bargaining, a reimbursible state-mandated cost, but instead proposed that an imputed cost be funded on a formula basis.

Yet another area of increased interdependence concerned personnel policies. SB 154 (1978) prohibited local governments receiving state bail-out funds from granting pay increases to their employees; Governor Brown insisted that state employees also would receive no pay raises. When court decisions struck down the prohibition against local-government pay increases and most granted them, pressure for state-employee increases mounted, and the legislature enacted a retroactive (lump-sum) raise. The governor vetoed the measure, the legislature overrode the veto, an appeals court ruled it unconstitutional, and the state supreme court finally ruled it constitutional. In mid–1981, some legislators complained whenever a local jurisdiction gave its employees a pay raise greater than that state employees were granted in the FY 1981–1982 state budget. The question of equivalence in personnel practices among state and local governments in areas where the state plays an increased fiscal role was bound to arise.

Finally, interdependence was increased by the political uncertainty that is so important in the world of California governments after Proposition 13. The uncertainty is derived in part from the possibility of more initiatives that may constrain revenues or otherwise shape policy choices (remember that Jarvis qualified an initiative to permanently and fully index the personal-income tax, and he talked of another to "straighten out" public pensions). Uncertain also are the longer-term potentials and pitfalls of the nontraditional approaches to the achievement of public purposes now being explored (such as the issues of more or less regulation, or public-private joint ventures). And, of course, the election of Ronald Reagan will bring changes in the federal government's posture toward state and local government (and the certainty of reduced federal grants-in-aid), adding further state-and-local political uncertainty and interdependence.

The Ascendant Legislature

Of all the governmental institutions in the state, the legislature must be credited with having the largest causal effect in regard to Proposition 13, for it could not respond effectively to mounting pressure for tax relief, as analyzed in chapter 3. Similarly, of all California governmental institutions, the legislature was most critical after Proposition 13. As analyzed in chapter 4, it reshaped the intergovernmental fiscal system of the state. Powerful before passage of the Jarvis-Gann Initiative, the legislature was even more ascendant afterward.

The basis of the legislature's power is largely constitutional. Though the governor can propose, cajole, and veto, only the legislature can change tax laws or substantially modify the system of local governments. The one major exception to legislative domination is the initiative. The legislature added to its constitutional powers as a result of the reforms that made it essentially a full-time body. Since being a legislator required more time, and provided increased financial livelihood, individuals were attracted to the legislature as a career. To further their careers (and to solve problems, do good, and so on), legislators expanded the scope of legislative activity. Moreover, Governor Brown's style of intense commitment to a few issues provided a vacuum for legislative policy initiative. During his two bids for the presidency in 1976 and 1980, Brown was even less a presence in state policymaking.

The simplest way to understand post-Proposition 13 policymaking in the state of California is to focus on how the legislature gave highest priority to solving its own problems. More charitably, but no more accurately, the legislature solved others' problems within its own constraints. It must be remembered that although Proposition 13 cut local property-tax revenues, it also had immediate, powerful effects on the legislature. Previously developed state policies and programs that assumed the earlier fiscal capacity of local government had to be reconstructed. A simple way to do so was to try to heal local governments' fiscal wounds sufficiently so that the old policies and programs could continue. The alternative would have been a free-for-all of interest groups clamoring for relief from the legislature. The state surplus provided the means for fiscal relief to local governments. Equally important, the legislature needed to accommodate the changed political mood that threatened defeat of incumbents (a few were defeated), and more fiscal-constraint initiatives (one was passed). Drawing on the state surplus was the obvious mechanism to solve these problems.

However, as chapter 4 argued, the legislature protected the state budget and state employment more than it did those of cities and counties. Moreover, over four budget cycles, it sought to reduce the disruption caused by Propositions 13 and 4 and fiscal relief to local governments to its core processes. The budget cycle is key to the functioning of the legislature, and it is not surprising to any student of organization theory that the legislature soon tried to get the bail-out into the ongoing budget process so as to disturb it as little as possible (Kirlin 1981b). By the spring of 1981, the legislature had largely accomplished that objective. Although more change may be needed if the California economy falters, if another fiscal initiative passes, or if federal cuts in grants are larger than anticipated, the pattern seen between 1978 and 1981 should not change.

Moreover, while institutional problems of the legislature were being solved, individual legislators continued in much the same manner as they had prior to June, 1978. As suggested earlier, the general policy tone of the body remained liberal. Legislators continued to fine-hone their systems of generating campaign contributions. In the 1980 general election, major-party candidates received $15,337,666 in campaign contributions, of which $13,887,095 was itemized as to source in reports to the Fair Political Practices Commission because it was received in amounts of $100 or more. Fully

Table 5-1

Financing of Major-Party Campaigns for the California Legislature, November 1980

Legislative Body	Number of Candidates	Average Amount of Contributions (dollars)	Itemized Contributions $100 or Over (percentages)	
			From Outside District	From State Political Action Committes
Senate				
Incumbents	19	108,544	82	55
Nonincumbents	20	68,893	74	41
Winners	20	126,504	79	52
Losers	19	47,900	74	42
Assembly				
Incumbents	65	93,757	78	47
Nonincumbents	87	62,205	73	35
Winners	79	102,505	77	44
Losers	73	52,048	73	36

Source: Compiled from: State of California, Fair Political Practices Commission, *Sources of Contributions to California State Legislative Candidates for the November 4, 1980 General Election* (Sacramento: Fair Political Practices Commission, 1981).

77 percent of these itemized funds came from outside of the districts in which the candidates were running and 43 percent came from state-level political-action committees (FPPC 1981). Table 5-1 shows the amounts and sources of itemized contributions to incumbents and nonincumbents and winning and losing candidates of major parties. Incumbents raised, on average, 50 to 60 percent more in campaign contributions than did nonincumbents. Winners received from two to two-and-one-half times the contributions of losers. Importantly, incumbents and winners both received proportionately greater contributions from outside of their districts and from state-level political-action committees than did nonincumbents and losers. Most important of all, the pattern for all candidates was of successful adaptation to a campaign-financing system based overwhelmingly on special-interest groups rather than on jurisdictions.

One of the fundamental causes and consequences of the ascendancy of the legislature is derived from this pattern of campaign financing. Legislators (and aspirants to that office) need special-interest groups for campaign financing, and special-interest groups need legislators to advance or protect their interests. Both sides of the campaign-financing process have compelling incentives to strengthen the legislature. Neither Proposition 13, nor any other issue, stands much chance of altering this dynamic. Instead, every new opportunity is turned to the use of the campaign-funding process. All that is required to do so is the creation of continued dependence of the interest group on action of the legislature. Chapter 6 returns to some of the issues raised at the outset of this volume concerning the impact of such dynamics on the political system itself.

6 **Alternatives**

Proposition 13 and related events have had, and will continue to have, a substantial impact on the state of California. Though not all of the fiscal limits adopted by thirty other states in recent years will have as great an impact, neither will the status quo be likely to prevail in most of those states. In the context of the general trend since the mid-1970s to shrink the public-sector budget and of the agenda of President Reagan (especially his successes on the budget and taxation in 1981), the fiscal trends and policy orientations that dominated from mid-1960 to mid-1970 are being severely dislocated. If further evidence is needed that a period of instability concerning what government should be doing and how it should do it is occurring, a review of events in most other industrialized democracies over the last decade should be convincing. Such a review would also suggest that the appropriate response to this instability is a very hotly contested issue. For example, Prime Minister Thatcher of Great Britain seeks to cut the public-sector budget and revitalize private industry. The fact that she continues in office despite great difficulty in achieving her announced policy objectives, and despite deteriorating economic performance, is powerful testimony to the intellectual poverty of the opposition Labor party and evidence of the link between theory and policy to be further explored. Mitterrand, France's newly elected Socialist president, advocates an almost diametrically opposed set of remedies, including nationalization of banking and some industries. Scandinavian nations remain largely committed to the welfare state but are confronting severe fiscal constraints and groping for responsive policies.

As suggested in chapter 1, the reason the Fiscal Limits Movement is a critical event for American society is that it requires a political response and policy redirection of sufficient magnitude as to have substantial long-term impact on our society. How substantial might the impact be? Probably at least as great as that resulting from the Great-Society programs of the mid-1960s, perhaps as great as that of the Progressives on governmental structures or that of the New Deal on the size and scope of the national government's role in managing the economy of the nation. It is critical to understand that the lasting impacts of fiscal limits in this nation (and others) will arise less from the limits themselves or from any diminution of services that may result, but more from the responses developed to them. The fundamental reason for this is that those responses define the capacity of political systems to act in the future.

Such a statement will be novel to some, repugnant to others, and not-at-all exceptional to yet others. More frequently of late the adequacy of our political system has been judged by the effectiveness and efficiency with which it delivers services or the equality it achieves for citizens. Effective and efficient service delivery and equality are important, but their achievement is not the critical role of government. Government is the institution with singular obligations to facilitate societal choice making and action. Its continuing ability to make choices and to act are the dominant dimensions by which its performance should be judged. Choices and action at any particular moment often revolve around service delivery or efforts to achieve equality. But an evaluation of the adequacy of a governmental choice or action is simply an evaluation and should not be confused with the ongoing capacity of the political system to again choose and act. This distinction is more than definitional nit-picking. Chapter 2 argued that the consequences of policies adopted (usually in the name of equality of access) to reform political institutions and to deliver an expanded menu of services in the 1960s and 1970s, affected the political system itself, largely negatively in terms of its capactiy to choose and act. The capacity-to-choose-and-act standard has deep roots in Western political philosophy, was the overriding concern of the framers of the United States Constitution, and finds modern expression in several important critiques of the functioning of the United States political system (Janowitz 1976; Schon 1971; Ladd 1978; Schattschneider 1960; Wolin 1968; Presthus 1978). This chapter argues for such a capacity orientation to political systems, and advances a heuristic model of the design of political institutions and of policymaking.

Seven Frameworks of Response to Fiscal Limitation

The argument for an approach based on capacity to choose and act is easiest to comprehend, to evaluate, and even, perhaps, to accept, in comparison with other possible alternatives for structuring responses to fiscal constraint. Six other alternatives are presented and evaluated. Each of the seven alternatives is based in some understanding of the causes of fiscal limits, has a model of a preferred political system, advances proposals as to how to respond to fiscal limits, and is characterized by certain advantages and disadvantages. The several alternatives are compared on these five dimensions; the comparison is summarized in table 6-1. A discussion of each alternative framework of response follows. Some speak more immediately to fiscal limits; others intend to address larger perceived inadequacies of the political system.

Table 6–1
Alternative Responses to Fiscal Limitation

Responses/Positions	Perceived Cause of Fiscal Limits	Attributes of Preferred Political System	Proposals	Advantages	Difficulties
Governmental structure					
Grudging accommodation	Uninformed citizens; mismanaged public sector.	"What used to be"; expanding public sector.	Wait, outmaneuver; ease limits.	An old familiar game.	Tends to underestimate pressure for change; over time weakens political system.
Centralization of political power	Ineffective, inefficient, unjust political system.	Uniformity of services; professionalization.	Strengthen central government.	Fits long-term dynamic.	Exacerbates problems of access to political system.
Reallocation of functions	Inappropriate allocation of functions leading to poor, costly policies.	Neat, rational allocation of service-providing responsibilities.	Reallocate functions, usually according to some rational criteria.	Challenges trend to mindless centralization.	Little agreement on how to reallocate functions; previous such reforms often failures.
Rebalance public versus private					
Tilt toward private sector	Government too large and intrusive.	Vital private sector; limited, strong public sector.	Cut government revenues and expenditures.	Openly advocates fiscal limits.	Can be naive; tends toward a static view.
Tilt toward public sector	Conservative sentiment in electorate.	Equality; expanded public sector.	Strengthen national government, expand public sector.	Appeals to culturally important values concerning equality.	Has lost intellectual power; the supporting economic theory under challenge.
Revitalizing the political system					
"Re-form" Political Institutions	Deficiencies in political institutions	Effectiveness; efficiency; capacity to govern.	Institutional reform; revive political parties.	Familiar-sounding proposals; emphasis on political capacity.	"Reforms" have misfired before; hard to sell.
Reconceptualization of the political system	Poor theory and poor structures lead to a weak political system.	Capacity to learn, act, adapt.	Better theory; reemphasize jurisdictions; keep value of political system itself uppermost.	A sharp break with present dynamics, yet familiar and deeply held values.	Counter to long-term dynamics of centralization, interest groups, and technocracy.

The seven alternatives are grouped into three categories of response: those that emphasize governmental structure, those that seek to change the balance between the public and private sectors of society, and those that seek to revitalize the political system. Though advocates of each of the alternatives may be found, some are commonly more openly advanced as normatively preferable (such as reassigning governmental functions) while others are frequently discussed in descriptive terminology (such as the belief that political power is becoming centralized). However, to describe a phenomenon and then to act in accordance with that description is to exercise a normative choice concerning what values to pursue. Political institutions and policies are social constructions that change over time, always as the result of human choice. Accordingly, the normative dimensions of these institutions and policies are emphasized here, for it is on these normative dimensions that choice among the alternatives must be made.

Grudging Accommodation

One of the simplest and most widely embraced views (at least when the phenomenon of fiscal limits was first experienced) held that the appropriate response was the absolute minimum possible, that is, grudging accommodation. In California, an example of this perspective was the governor's Commission on Government Reform. Appointed in June, 1978 and issuing its final report in January, 1979, the commission gave the opinion that revenues to replace those lost to Proposition 13 might well have to be raised (1979, p.36). The need for replacement revenue was, it must be noted, not an automatic conclusion, but argued to be a likely necessity if possible economies and the growth rates of remaining state and local revenues were not sufficient to meet needs. Moreover, the behavior of the state legislature, analyzed in chapter 4, could be interpreted as consonant with this perspective. State activities were protected, efforts made to blunt the full possible impact of Proposition 4, Proposition 9 was fought (and defeated), and the discontinuity posed by Proposition 13 was, over time, accommodated rather fully into the ongoing annual budget cycle.

Centralization of Political Power

Samuel Beer explains changes in the American political system in terms of a movement toward centralization caused, virtually inexorably, by modernization, looking "to modernization as the principal source of the changing division of power between levels of government" (1974, p. 51). He analyzes phases of modernity, finding that the overall trend is toward centralization of political authority in response to the emergence of large, complex networks of social interaction. Development of the intergovernmental system is traced through the "pork-barrel" distribution politics of the Jacksonian era, the "spillover coalition" regulatory politics of the Republican period from the end of the Civil War to the New Deal, the "class coalition" redistributive politics of the New-Deal era, to the technocratic "instrumental politics of the post-war period" (1974 p. 57). Beer's most interesting analysis concerns the present period of technocratic politics, a primary feature of which he argues is the shift of the initiative in policymaking from the economic and social environment to government itself. Moreover, much of the policymaking in this system entails development of new governmental initiatives to remedy or offset negative spillovers of earlier public policies.

Beer expects technocratic politics to be "pure bureaucratic politics . . . concerned with means rather than ends" (1974, p. 77). He predicts that professional bureaucratic complexes will coalesce around functional areas, and the central core of professionals will have close integration through all levels of government. Analysis will play a large part in policy development, and the generality of scientific knowledge will encourage centralization of power of innovation processes (1974, pp. 79–80). The role of subordinate governments will become that of "planning and control," defined largely as integrating functionally specific federal policies, and "mobilization of consent," intended to variously "educate the clientele, win their cooperation and endow them with some real power of influencing outputs" (1974, p. 85). Beer's apparent acceptance of the inevitability of this scenario is striking. He laments the prospect of uncontrollable public bureaucracies "mastering man," but he concludes that this is "merely . . . the fortune of all highly developed modern societies" (1974, p. 91). Beer accepts the equation of government with service delivery and sees no alternative to an elite technocracy of policy analysts pursuing synoptic rationality.

California's experience with Proposition 13 is explicable from this perspective also. Chapters 4 and 5 detailed how power and discretion flowed to the state from local government, and how, within the state government, the legislature's power grew as a result of its constitutional centrality in developing a response to fiscal limits. Levine and Posner (1979) argued that austerity at the state- and local-government levels would encourage centralization of power at the national-government level. Centralization is clearly one alternative response to fiscal constraints.

The two previous frameworks of response to fiscal limits are usually offered as descriptive analyses; the remaining five proposals are directly normative, and seek to remedy perceived problems in the political system.

Reallocation of Functions

The Advisory Commission on Intergovernmental Relations (ACIR) has
long advocated a conscious reallocation of functions among units of the
intergovernmental system. In 1976, for example, they argued that ad hoc
functional assignment led to four strains in the governmental system: service inefficiency, service inequities, ineffective delivery, and inadequate
citizen involvement and political accountability (1976, p. 111). To remedy
these perceived inadequacies, the ACIR advanced four criteria (1976, p.
115):

1. Economic effecency. Functions should be assigned to jurisdictions:
   a. that are large enough to realize economies of scale and small enough
      not to incur diseconomies of scale;
   b. that are willing to provide alternative service offerings to their citi-
      zens and specific services within a price range and level of effective-
      ness acceptable to local citizenry; and
   c. that adopt pricing policies for their functions whenever possible.
2. Fiscal equity. Appropriate functions should be assigned to jurisdictions:
   a. that are large enough to encompass the cost and benefits of a func-
      tion or that are willing to compensate other jurisdictions for the ser-
      vice costs imposed or for benefits received by them; and
   b. that have adequate fiscal capacity to finance their public service re-
      sponsibilities and that are willing to implement measures that ensure
      interpersonal and interjurisdictional fiscal equity in the perfor-
      mance of a function.
3. Political accountability. Functions should be assigned to jurisdictions
   that are controllable by, accessible to, and accountable to their residents in the performance of their public-service responsibilities.
4. Administrative effectiveness. Functions should be assigned to jurisdictions:
   a. that are responsible for a wide variety of functions and that can
      balance competing functional interests;
   b. that encompass a geographic area adequate for effective perfor-
      mance of a function;
   c. that explicitly determine the goals and means of discharging public-
      service responsibilities and that periodically reassess program goals
      in light of performance standards;
   d. that are willing to pursue intergovernmental policies for promoting
      interlocal functional cooperation and reducing interlocal functional
      conflict; and
   d. that have adequate legal authority to perform a function and rely on
      it in administering the function.

More recently, the ACIR reiterated the same theme, making its first
recommendation for improving the operation of the intergovernmental
system the "decongestion" of the federal grant system, to occur by reallocation of functional responsibilities (1980b, p. 37).

Reform advocates in California pursued similar visions. The California Council on Intergovernmental Relations classified services according to whether they provided individual benefits, group or societal benefits, or largely individual benefits that had spillover benefits to society, and then developed criteria for policy choice, for financing, and for administration of services (State of California, Council on Intergovernmental Relations 1970, pp. 6, 25). The Local Government Reform Task Force, also appointed by then-governor Reagan, sought to make local governments more responsive to citizens, to encourage efficient service delivery, and to provide effective problem-solving arenas (State of California, Local Government Reform Task Force 1974, pp. 2, 45).

Regardless of its appeal to reform advocates, promulgation of principles and criteria for allocation of functions among governments has had little actual effect. Change occurs almost routinely in service delivery and in governing mechanisms, and the dimensions identified in criteria development—efficiency, equity, responsiveness, and of whether individuals or collectivities benefit—have been considered by those making changes, but no comprehensive reallocation has been accomplished. Some might attribute this lack of success to the staying power of entrenched interest groups. This explanation should not be dismissed lightly, but its credibility is challenged both by the magnitude of changes that ultimately occur, albeit in piecemeal fashion, and by the weaknesses ineherent in the criteria-development enterprise.

At root, criteria development is based on the beliefs that change occurs from the top down in a comprehensive retructuring according to rational principles, that functions may be treated separately, that nongovernmental coproducers may be ignored, and that government's role is that of service provider. These are questionable premises. Moreover, no evidence exists that the present allocation of functions among state and local governments in California is gravely flawed, and no evidence exists that voters (before or after Proposition 13 desired a reshuffling of functions. Although available evidence suggests that the national government has centralized functions that would be better undertaken at the state and local level (ACIR 1980b), little agreement exists as to how any reallocation of functions should occur. In 1981, for example, Congress rejected some of President Reagan's proposals to create block grants giving states more discretion, and the president and the nation's state and local officials showed clear differences of opinion as to who should undertake what functions, especially in regard to welfare.

Tilt toward the Private Sector

A common explanation for the passage of Proposition 13, and for the general movement toward fiscal limits is the desire to reduce the revenues and

and expenditures of government. As discussed earlier, Boskin (1979) argued that citizens might well support fiscal limits because of strains on their economic situations and apprehension that the economy would continue to worsen. Shannon has analyzed the sources of growth and decline in the state and local public sectors. He also provides a concise summary of what advocates (whom he terms conservatives) hope to achieve by reducing the revenues and expenditures of the public sector (1981, pp. 19–20):

> Because of their efficiency and private market concerns, conservatives view the great slowdown in state-local spending as a most welcome development that was long overdue. They argue that the domestic public sector has steadily gained weight for decades and it will now have to stop gaining and hopefully slim down a little. They are encouraged by the fact that first local governments, then state governments, and finally the federal aid programs have been put on more restrictive diets.

> They argue that this leaner revenue diet will not do serious harm to the health of state and local governments or to their constituencies. On the contrary, they predict that, as a result of the taxpayer's revolt and now Reagan's New Federalism state and local governments will soon become more trim and less dependent on Washington than they have been for years. This, in turn, should make states and localities more accountable, innovative, and efficient providers of public services. They point out that the far-reaching civil rights and reapportionment reforms of recent years should allay fears of those who are concerned about the equitable treatment of the poor and the minority groups at the state and local levels. Finally, they contend that the federal government can best improve the fortunes of poor people and poor cities by restoring the nation to economic health.

Tilt toward the Public Sector

Not all citizens of California are pleased with the impact of Proposition 13, nor are all citizens of the nation pleased with constraint first of local and state fiscal resources, and then under Reagan, of the federal government's revenues.

A dilemma for some policymakers is how to address problems, without a large public budget. In the spring of 1980, Donna E. Shalala, Assistant Secretary for Policy Research and Development in the U.S. Department of Housing and Urban Development in the Carter presidency, lamented: "[I regret] . . . that I was born too late to be an assistant secretary in the Johnson administration—any administration in which budgets and the role of government were expanding. No one at the Maxwell School taught me the politics of scarcity. I honestly don't know how to solve the problems of our great cities without spending or leveraging significant public monies." (1980).

For others, the movement toward fiscal limits implies a conservative or neoconservative philosophy they find distasteful. William M. Roth, a long-time liberal Democrat, wrote of his experience on the Commission on Government Reform (in the section offering supplementary views to its *Final Report*) as follows (1979, p. 102):

> The successful passage of Proposition 13 burst upon the State and national scene like a flaming meteor, prophesying of things to come. A New Jerusalem of governmental restraint was to be built. In Commission discussions of alternate methods of financing public needs, some members argued it was forbidden to consider any deviation from the mandate of the electorate (and various individuals had various interpretations of what that mandate was). The mystic aura of untouchability that hung over this particular political message tended to hinder consideration of vitally needed improvements in the tax system itself—i.e., reducing hidden subsidies in our complicated and extensive system of sales and property tax exemptions. Any suggestion that certain aspects of Proposition 13 could be improved—such as remedying the inequities it will develop with future turnover of properties—was derided as an insult to the perfection of the amendment. Rational discussion was inhibited by political awe.
>
> Such a blind allegiance to one element of the voters' concerns overlooks others. The American people, as I read history, have been deeply concerned with social justice. From the beginning of the Republic, citizens from all economic strata have, intermittently but steadily, pushed forward the frontiers of social equity. In no way do I sense that this forward motion will be stopped by the fact that those very people who generously supported a more just society have become concerned not only with the cost of the effort, but by its increasing bureaucratization. The voters are smart enough to distinguish between objectives and processes.
>
> Therefore, I am concerned that our report, good as it is, does not carry a sufficient tone of social urgency. We are an affluent people and, in spite of inflation, these are affluent times. We are a great nation and, in times of peace, can afford whatever we legitimately need. Why, then, is there hunger—actual hunger—among the elderly poor in California; permanent unemployment and underemployment among the minority poor; inadequate funding of the brains and talent that alone will make the good things happen in this State? Any report that deals with the reform of government should make the point that the objectives of public policy must, if it is to remain in the American tradition, reflect these fundamental human concerns as well as the managerial ones of excessive costs and institutional fatigue. The thrust of this document should address itself more eloquently to these important social and political imperatives.

Liberals seeking to expand the public sector often link fiscal limits with conservative political sentiment. Though such a link is tenuous in explaining the vote for Proposition 13, as discussed in chapter 3, it is plausible for the Reagan presidency in which pursuit of a conservative political agenda is reducing federal taxing and spending. Arthur Schlesinger, Junior, has written bitingly of what he believes the dangers of the Reagan administration to be: that its laissez-faire neoconservatism will be so successful in cutting services and income transfers to the poor and needy that class warfare may occur (*Wall Street Journal* June 2, 1981, p. 22). Regardless of the accuracy of this prognosis, the liberal conviction that the domestic public sector should expand is unlikely to be fulfilled in the early 1980s. Beyond the obvious facts that the movement toward fiscal constraint is broader than the Reagan presidency and its bases broader than neoconservatism, the liberal pro-public-sector position is weakened by growing doubts about the policy effectiveness of its supporting Keynesian economic theory.

"Re-reform" Political Institutions

Yet another alternative response to fiscal limitation is to *"re-reform"* political institutions. The somewhat awkward term "re-reform" captures a core point in much of this line of argument. Earlier reform efforts are perceived as a major cause of the inadequacies of the political system, of which fiscal limits are sometimes seen as a corollary and other times as symptomatic of those weaknesses.

James Sundquist (1980) of the Brookings Institution is a fairly typical proponent of this alternative. Sundquist is somewhat distinctive in his focus on the national government and specifically on the need to strengthen presidential leadership capacity. In contrast, the Advisory Commission on Intergovernmental Relations (1980b) focuses on the whole intergovernmental system (which they judge to be too dependent on the national government), and the editors of the *National Journal,* in their special issue entitled "Can We Govern?" (January 19, 1980), define the problem not only in terms of weak presidential leadership and an unwieldy intergovernmental system, but also in terms of poor policies concerning the federal government's role in the economy.

Sundquist (1980) argues that the crisis of confidence in government revealed in citizen surveys is caused by voters' experience of electing presidents who do not have programs that address their central problems. Nor have winners been able to implement any consistent programs. He finds the causes of these weaknesses in the disintegration of political parties, haphazard presidential selection (largely the result of reforms that reduced the influence of party elites and caused a proliferation of direct primaries), rejection of presidential leadership by Congress, limitations on congressional leadership, and a deterioration of administrative competence. Logically, his proposals address each of these weaknesses, although he believes little can be done to revive political parties.

Reconceptualization of the Political System

The final alternative is paradoxically both elusive and achievable. A starting point in exploration of this alternative is to return briefly to the four-sector model of political processes advanced in chapter 1. The development and change of theories, particularly regarding policy strategies, was identified as one of the four elements of this model. It is the element of the model that "drives" the other three (electoral, fiscal, and institutional), not in the sense that it fully controls them, nor that no other factor affects political systems but in the sense that it is the element of the model that can be most consciously manipulated. Moreover, as political theory changes, institutions will be redesigned, the size of the public purse changed, and political behavior affected.

From this perspective, *theory,* or how we perceive public problems, conceptualize responsive public policies, and think about the design of political institutions, is tremendously powerful. No perception, no choice, no action occurs without the filter, bias, and power of theory and language. This approach to developing responses to fiscal limits is elusive both because it is abstract and discussed at a different plane than much political discourse, and because it is threatening, since it forces conscious examination of values and beliefs often deeply held.

However, one of the interesting dimensions of periods of change in political systems is the ferment of ideas. Indeed, there could be no change without such ferment. Competition among ideas concerning the public sector was very evident in the late 1970s to early 1980s. Ronald Reagan and Tip O'Neil hold different theories and speak different political languages. They perceive different problems, believe in different policy strategies, pursue different policies. Margaret Thatcher and Francois Mitterand are even further apart in the theories they employ; and Howard Jarvis shares few ideas with Jerry Brown even after Brown's conversion to Proposition 13. At another level, macroeconomic theory is hotly debated, with tremendous impact on public policymaking and on society. It is quite probable that none of the theories associated with the individual political figures mentioned will come to fully dominate policymaking in their respective arenas. In particular, the narrow neoconservative proscription of simply cutting down on government and encouraging the private sector appears to be too simplistic to become fully ascendant, but so too are the caricatured versions of New-Deal liberalism being advanced by some liberals. Eventually some body of theory will emerge to dominate policy choice and the design of political institutions, only to be ultimately challenged as it proves unable to accommodate new demands placed on the political system. The contemporary period of conflict over theories is an opportune time to think rather systematically about these choices, the task undertaken here.

Before initiating such consideration, it is important to note that citizens of the United States, though often critical of the performance of political leaders, are less critical of political processes and institutions, and are optimistic that the performance of a political system can be improved. Citizens are supportive of an improved political system; without such support, the task of change would be vastly more difficult. A nationwide *Los Angeles Times* poll taken during the 1980 presidential election found that 70 percent of the respondents believed the nominating process to be basically sound, and 62 percent believed the political system also to be basically sound. In comparison, 71 percent judged business and industry and 49 percent the judicial system to be basically sound (*Los Angeles Times,* January 27, 1980). On the issue of expectations of what the political system could be, a 1978 Harris survey asked respondents two questions: "Do we have a government that fits these listed characteristics?" and "Is it possible to have such a government?" Responses for four characteristics are illustrated in table 6–2.

To reconceptualize a political system, one must begin with some definition of that system. Though many discussions emphasize jurisdictions as the unit of analysis (such as Sundquist 1980), the intergovernmental system as a whole is the focus here. This focus is justified by recognition that the federal character of our political institutions is one of their major defining attributes, by a perception that the relationships among jurisdictions have changed dramatically in the last two decades, and by a belief that the trends evident in those changes are injurious to effective functioning of the polity.

In developing a heuristic model of the intergovernmental system that could serve as a basis for reconceptualization, an immediate choice concerns expectations about the power of rationality and the predictability of social systems. This is the familiar choice between synoptic and strategic rationality (Lindblom 1977, pp. 314–329) or between center-periphery and learning-system models of innovation (Schon 1971). If one holds to the position that our capacity for rationality is high, that social systems are predictable, and that we can effectively translate policy initiatives into achievements, the most appropriate heuristic model of the intergovernmental system would be a series of hierarchical bureaucracies. More inclusive bureaucracies would relate to less inclusive as central headquarters to a field office. Evaluations of governmental performance would seek information with which to perfect policymaking and implementation through improvements in centralized choice making and bureaucratic implementation. Conformity to centralized decision making would be sought, and only "planned variations" would be legitimate, and even those would be viewed as demonstrations, the evaluation of which would ultimately allow definitive policymaking. The federal government would urge "capacity building" for local governments, seeking to make them more perfect administrative instru-

Table 6-2
Polled Attitudes toward Government, 1978
(percentages)

Theoretical Government Characteristics	Have	Do Not Have	Possible	Not Possible
Almost wholly free of corruption and payoffs	10	84	48	45
Best people are attracted to serve in public life	18	69	68	22
The good of the country is placed above special interests	26	61	76	16
Public officials really care what happens to people	38	48	81	12

Source: 1978 Harris poll quoted in James L. Sundquist, "The Crisis of Competence in Government" in Joseph A. Pechman, ed., *Setting National Priorities: Agenda for the 1980s* (Washington, D.C. The Brookings Institution, 1980), p. 537.

ments of central policy, and more auditable. Although presented here so starkly as to be a caricature, this orientation dominates policymaking processes in the United States and is the foundation for much policy-analytic work. The urge to pursue synoptic rationality has impact even if the goal is never achieved. Language, policy and organizational design, and expectations of officials and citizens reflect the bias.

Alternatively, the intergovernmental system is approached through a heuristic model that conceptualizes decision making and action capability as widely dispersed, a model that doubts the capacity for extensive a priori rationality, the predictability of social systems, and the ability to achieve intentions by changing behaviors. Schon (1971) is a well-known advocate of this perspective, but his work is weakened by its apolitical character, which results in idealization of functionally specific networks dominated by professionals and not held accountable through any political processes. In several publications, Lindblom has explored alternatives to synoptic rationality, expanding conceptualization from a fairly simple incremental model (Braybrooke and Lindblom 1963), through mechanisms of mutual adjustment (1965), to his recent formulation of strategic rationality, encompassing a family of approaches premised on recognition of limitations of human intellectual capacities "and the consequent need for an intellectual strategy to guide an inevitably incomplete analysis" (1977, p. 314).

The two contrasting approaches to rationality—synoptic or strategic—differ on several dimensions of central importance to the intergovernmental system: fundamentally in methods of problem definition and in expectations concerning human intellectual capacity, and consequently in institutional design, policy strategies, and evaluation activities. Table 6–3 contrasts the two approaches on these five dimensions. The two approaches to rationality yield very different approaches to institutional design, policy strategies, and evaluation activities. Given the beliefs that problems are clear and permanent, and that individual intellectual capabilities are great, or that the capacity of organizations and institutions for rational action is high, these values carry through into the approach to action, encouraging institutions, policies, and evaluations premised on being able to correctly diagnose the problem, develop appropriate policies and institutions, implement policies effectively, evaluate the consequences of these actions, and, if necessary, change policies and institutions in response to the evaluations. The alternative starting point similarly influences action, with almost diametrically opposed orientations as to what should be done.

What heuristic model of the intergovernmental system would be appropriate given a presumption that synoptic rationality is impossible to achieve and that, indeed, action based on its premises is likely to be not only ineffectual but actually dysfunctional? Several authors provide clues in this effort. Landau emphasizes redundancy; overlapping and duplicative jurisdictions provide capacity for error sensing and action; and the virtues of "a truly messy system" are exalted (1974, p. 188). LaPorte advocates recognition of policy implementation as error making, suggesting that planning be redefined as learning. As to the specific values that should guide institutional design and policymaking, he argues for reversibility and functional redundancy (1975, pp. 347–351). Evaluation should encourage "error exploring rather than error camouflaging, error embracing rather than error punishing" (1975, p. 352). Wildavsky (1979, pp. 212–236) trenchantly observes that these exhortations directly contravene the central values of organizations: to be stable, predictable, and controlling. Organization and evaluation are said to be incompatible.

Wildavsky's own prescriptions relevant to the political system are not clearly stated but must be teased from his discussion of policy analysis. He not only advocates variety and reversibility, but also adds another dimension in his discussions of objectives and values (1979, pp. 392–406). Values are relevant first as the basis of citizenship, which requires that individuals trust the political system sufficiently to participate supportively; second as conventions, holding that not all is subject to possible change and constraining means; and third, as the basis for objectives. Wildavsky argues that objectives change, and that a critical requirement of an effective political system is that it allow objectives to change, providing both opportunity for wide learning and behavior change (such as pricing petroleum products at the world price so that citizens could comprehend and act, rather than subsidizing oil consumption, "protecting" citizens from the possibility of understanding and individual accommodation), and for leadership, in

Table 6-3
Synoptic and Strategic Approaches to Policymaking

Approach	Method of Problem Definition	Expectations concerning Human Intellectual Capacity	Approaches to Institutional Design	Preferred Policy Strategies	Approach to Evaluation Activities
Synoptic	Expects clarity, permanence.	Great, individually, organizationally, and institutionally.	"Once and for all"; hard to change; dominated by professionals; bureaucratic; statist; interventionist; vertical.	Directive; controlling; permanent; top-down hierarchical; monopolistic; narrow.	Seeks definitive universals; evaluation intended for use by central administrators; directed from the center; secrecy.
Strategic	Expects ill-definition, change.	Limited individually, organizationally and institutionally.	Temporary; malleable; open to influence; market; entrepreneurial; conservative; horizontal.	Facilitative; variation desirable; policy initiatives fragmented; reversible; broad.	Seeks partial insight; attentive to context and nuance; evaluation intended for wide use; evaluations originate at many locations; sharing.

which visions of the future may be defined and possibly achieved. What is needed is a political system that allows change in "terminal" public values while maintaining constancy in "instrumental" public values.

Learning and change require the ability to modify or terminate existing institutions and policies, a requirement already suggested to be difficult to meet. Biller (1976) has developed design considerations intended to make policy and organizational termination easier. His most general recommendation is to recognize that whereas organizations are premised on permanence, markets are premised on impermanent, temporary exchanges. Encouraging creation of markets and intervention in their workings may often achieve public purposes with less risk of permanence and irreversibility.

Another suggestion is to institutionalize the procedures of choice making and change rather than particular organizations and policies. Within organizations, matrix designs may be used, wherein the larger organization achieves permanence while project task forces are routinely created, act, and are terminated. Biller also suggests several institutions and policies that could be established to facilitate change and termination, including: savings banks; insurance policies; receivership referees; trust offices; salvage specialists; and marriage, divorce, and escrow brokerages. All are intended as mechanisms to routinize termination of existing policies and organizations, a precondition of the ability to learn and adapt, especially in a situation characterized by change and uncertainty.

Levine (1972) also urges the use of the market as a social institution for choice making and action, but cautions that in many areas social considerations are unlikely to be achieved through market exchanges. As other alternative institutional designs, he urges bureaucratic competition, breaking up the monopolies frequently given public bureaucracies (for an example, see Savas 1977a), and the development of explicit politico-bureaucratic bargaining arenas. Schultze (1970) has advanced similar proposals, urging the introduction of market competition into decisions about production of public goods, fuller imitations of the market in public programs, and partially regionalizing the federal budget.

A major concern of public-choice theorists is the consequence of alternative institutional designs, which are analyzed both formally, through axiomatic theory building, and empirically. Vincent Ostrom has written explicitly about the design of a "compound republic" (1971) and more broadly (1973) about the tension between a political system structured to serve hierarchical administrative agencies and a democratic administration of concurrent jurisdictions much like that envisaged by Madison in the Federalist Papers. Among the suggestions relevant to design of the intergovernmental system from this perspective are: the use of fragmentation and overlap to reduce participation costs and increase the likelihood of service provision attuned to the desires of citizens; the distinction among different types of goods (most importantly, among public and private goods) which provides a basis for choosing among alternative decision-rules; and the observation that public services should appropriately be provided by organizations of differing size.

In chapter 2, forces causing change in the intergovernmental system of the United States were reviewed. New policies that responded to the desire for increased equality and the demands of managing an advanced economy have dramatically altered intergovernmental relationships in the last fifteen years. One constant theme in this transformation was the elevation of functional-system requirements (such as health-services delivery, or environmental protection) over the needs of the political system. Administrative hegemony has not yet occurred, however, and some counterimpulses exist (such as general revenue sharing, or fiscal limits). Moreover, far from being characterized by uniform relationships among jurisdictions, as a simple federalism framework would suggest, the present system is characterized by exceptional variety in interrelationships, a consequence of differences among specific program areas. Table 6–4 presents a typology of these interrelationships (from Kirlin 1979, p. 87).

Table 6–4
Typology of Policy Strategies for National Policies in a Federal System

I. *Administrative Strategies*
    a. Entitlement programs, such as Medicaid, AFDC

    b. Categorical programs, such as Urban Mass Transportation grants

    c. Universalistic, specific regulations, such as Federal Management Circular 74–7, "Uniform Administrative Requirements for Grants-in-Aid to State and Local Governments"

II. *Organizational-Environment Strategies*
    a. Market interventions, such as housing subsidies

    b. Creation of bureaucratic markets, such as directly funded community-action programs

    c. Changing the system of legal rights, as in the Clean Air Act, 1977 amendments; civil rights acts

III. *Learning-System Strategies*
    a. Block-grant programs, such as Community Development Block Grants

    b. Create bargaining arenas under constraint, such as A–95 review, Section 208 Water Quality Planning

    c. General revenue-sharing programs that enhance local governments' fiscal capacity

    d. Noncentrally directed but centrally facilitated activities, such as state statutes that allow for development of alternative structures for delivery of local government services such as contracting out to another government or to a private firm.

The three classes of strategies illustrated in table 6–4 progress from those that have intentions of achieving a high degree of centralized control and nationwide equivalence of activity to those that have exactly the opposite intentions, of maximizing variety of activity while minimizing central control. Administrative strategies are based on synoptic rationality, requiring belief that objectives are clearly chosen, that causal links between desired objectives and policies are known, and that adopted policies may be implemented. The prototypical model for the administrative strategy is the hierarchical organization. Organizational-environment strategies, like the administrative strategy, has certainty concerning objectives and finds causality between policy and effect, but unlike administrative strategy relies on achieving the desired objective by directing organizational behaviors. Factors in the environment of organizations are changed in the expectation of eliciting desired behaviors from the target organizations. Interventions in market dynamics, intended to change organizational behavior through changing price signals, is the prototype here. In the third (learning-system) strategy, uncertainty exists concerning both objectives and means. In some cases, a policy objective may exist (such as environmental quality), but with uncertainty as to what this objective means in various instances and locales. In other cases, the objective is enhanced capacity of the intergovernmental system itself, with diffuse expectations that this will somehow improve policy achievement. The best prototype of this strategy may well be our federal system itself. This conclusion highlights the potential instability of a federal system in an era of pressures for national policymaking: administrative strategies can easily be inimical to a federal system; organizational-environment strategies are largely indifferent; and only learning-system strategies are congruent with sustaining such a political system.

Two normative arguments concerning design of an effective intergovernmental system may be drawn from the typology. First, a mixed intergovernmental system is desirable because it allows appropriate variety in intergovernmental relationships, enhancing the likelihood of successful action in various policy arenas. Second, the functioning of political jurisdictions (especially local governments) should be of greater importance than the achievement of any particular policy objective, because the destruction of viable jurisdictions disenfranchises citizens and reduces the range of possible policy strategies available to society.

Perhaps the most important observation that emerges from this discussion of the design of the intergovernmental system from a perspective sympathetic to strategic rationality is that the visions presented are significant departures from both dominant intellectual habit and present practice. Most of the authors discussed in this chapter are critical of the performance of the present intergovernmental system; the groping for new conceptualizations and theories is evident. No fully elaborated model of the intergovernmental system has been provided, even by loose usage of the term *model*. What has been provided by these authors are suggestions for more effective structure of the intergovernmental system.

The common themes that emerge include the following exhortations. To be effective an intergovernmental system should:

1. maintain widely dispersed capacity for societal choice making and action, while also maintaining capacity for focused joint action in critical areas;
2. encourage variation in institutional design, policy strategies, and methods of evaluation;
3. prefer policy strategies and institutional designs that are reversible, comprehensive, and nonmonopolistic;
4. use the many advantages that markets possess over administrative systems, when appropriate;
5. when possible, create decision situations in which individuals, organizations, and jurisdictions confront the consequences of alternative choices;
6. encourage the use of matrix organizational structures, of competition among bureaucracies, and of bargaining arenas;
7. ensure that value issues are clarified, allowed to change, and developed through leadership;
8. emphasize the context of policies in evaluations as much as their results, as the former factors are critical to others' abilities to innovate and probably to the results obtained;
9. seek to make evaluations error-exploring and embracing; and,
10. maintain the capacity of the system to make choices and to act, even at the cost of imperfections in achieving particular policy objectives.

Of course, not all will agree with this list of exhortations, nor with the values on which it is based. Lowi, for example, advocates the abolition of cities as jurisdictions (1979, pp. 261–263) and the development of juridical democracy characterized by strong congressional rule making that would in his estimate reduce administrative discretion, cooptation of power by private interests, and ineffectual policy (pp. 295–313). Lowi, however, is primarily judging the American political system by its ability to achieve racial equality. His indictment of its performance on that criterion is telling; though damning the performance of tens of thousands of local jurisdictions on the basis of a single case study (1979, pp. 238–258) is presumptuous. The counsel of Schattschneider (1960) is relevant here: democracy is a system that must work for people as they are; to attack the competence of the citizens, judging them unfit for democracy, is to build the premises of authoritarian regimes.

Lowi's position at least provides effective counterpoint to the values discussed in this analysis. These values may be briefly stated: political systems are most importantly institutions of choice making; jurisdictions are the critical building blocks of a democratic political system (whereas corporatism, the suppression of horizontal jurisdictional political activity in favor of vertical interest-oriented or policy-arena-oriented political activity, is ultimately technocratic, authoritarian, and paralyzing; Schmitter and Lehmbruch 1979); and many jurisdictions are preferable to few, as this encourages participation, increased flexibility, and lower costs of both governance and service provision.

Reprise

California voters approved Proposition 13 in June, 1978. At that time, such an action seemed an extraordinary event. It also appeared that the fiscal impact on California state and local governments would be dramatic. By mid–1981, as this is being written, neither perception can be judged to have been fully accurate. Most states now have some form of fiscal limitation, and state and local government revenues nationwide have been sharply constrained, partly because of fiscal limits, partly because of tax reductions, and partly because of declining federal grants. Federal expenditures, at least on domestic programs, are now being cut, as are federal taxes. The fiscal size of the public sector is being constrained. In the specific case of California, the total tax burden has decreased substantially, and expenditures have commonly declined slightly in constant dollars per capita, but their fall was cushioned by the state surplus. The distribution of the impact of these constraints is uneven in California; revenues of city governments were more sharply constrained than those of the state itself, for example. Over time, the provision of fiscal assistance to local governments has become more routinized, until it has become practically a normal part of the budget processes.

Because the state had a surplus and the constitutional powers needed to restructure the California state-local fiscal system, it had significant power advantages over local government after Proposition 13. Though that power was not abused, the state gained power over local governments as a result of Proposition 13. Moreover, the state legislature further developed and extended its domination of policymaking in the state. Power to reallocate revenue bases and fiscal assistance among local governments is the most important of the state's powers over local governments. The resulting instability in own-source revenues dramatically increased local-government dependence on state policy processes.

Possible responses to the changes occasioned by fiscal limits, and by fiscal constraint generally, range from grudging accomodation to extensive restructuring of the political and economic systems. Choice among these alternatives is based largely on perceptions of the causes of fiscal constraint and fiscal limits. The responses chosen will have more impact than the reduction in revenues themselves. As a consequence, the most careful consideration should be given to deciding how the political system of this nation should cope with fiscal constraint. To suggest the range of responses possible, and to illuminate the dimensions on which alternative responses could be evaluated, seven such alternatives were examined. The alternative advocated, that of reconceptualizing the political system, seeks to move discourse concerning the impact of fiscal limits and fiscal constraints away from revenues, expenditures, and services toward a focus on the sustained capacity of the political system itself to make choices and act effectively. From this perspective, the size of the public purse, and whether it shrinks or grows, is of less importance than is the design of political institutions and public policies. For those design decisions affect not only revenues, expenditures, and services, but most important, the capacity of the political system to choose and act.

The causes of Proposition 13 were more political than economic and the impact heavily political also. The greatest tragedy that could emerge from the current movement toward fiscal constraint would be the pursuit of responsive strategies that would further exacerbate the diminution of political capacity that was a major cause of the excesses that originally stimulated the movement toward fiscal constraint.

One undeniable impact of fiscal constraint has been to challenge the presumption of expanding public-sector revenues that was the premise of much policymaking at all three levels of government in the 1960s and 1970s. Policy strategies that were appropriate for an expanding public sector must now be reexamined; new policy proposals compete for reduced resources. Though initial responses to fiscal constraints may be to squeeze a bit here and there on established programs and policies, this posture is not sustainable if the fiscal constraint persists or deepens. Levine et al. (1981) provide empirical evidence of such a progression to more fundamental change in four local governments experiencing fiscal stress. As fiscal constraint persists, defense of the previous allocation of resources and of the old orthodoxy of permissible policy strategies becomes ever more difficult, restricting accommodation to changing circumstances and opportunities.

To choose and to act differently requires new theory and new language. What was not before perceived as possible policy must become so perceived. This has been the pattern of change in the political system in the past, and it will remain so. Labor's right to collective bargaining, individual civil rights, or the concept that protection of the environment should enter into virtually any decision affecting our physical surroundings were once not perceived or were even rejected as policy choices. Similar changes will be required as societal responses to fiscal constraint on the public sector are developed.

The explicit discussion of the relationships among language, theory, and action that follows seeks to at least partially unravel the process by which new responses to fiscal constraint will be elaborated. The discussion develops partially in opposition to the more-common model of interest-group dominated policy processes, arguing that the importance of language and theory in guiding policy choice has been underappreciated by both policymakers and analysts.

Language, Theory, and Action

A common model of political processes is based on interest groups. In this model, interest groups seek public policies of some benefit to their members (Olson 1965), and officials seek to build coalitions of interest groups in order to acquire the resources needed to remain in power (Cury and Wade 1968). Such reasoning has been applied to the generation of pressure for fiscal constraint and responsive policymaking by jurisdictions (Shefter 1977; Levine et al. 1981). This model has considerable explanatory power; the analysis of campaign contributions to the California legislature presented in chapter 5 provided evidence of the exchange process in that context.

However, such a model may have less explanatory power in times of more fundamental change in established patterns of policymaking. Indeed, Olson (1977) believes that one of the consequences that results from the mobilization and politicization of increasing numbers of interest groups over time is that they become barriers to change. In a case such as fiscal constraint, this model suggests that initial attempts will be made to maintain the existing coalition of interests, and when that is no longer possible, to reduce resources going to a weak interest group, essentially reducing the size of the coalition. This is the model of retrenchment developed by Levine et al. (1981), which they found only imperfectly explained what happened in the four local governments they analyzed, since more managerial decision making occurred than the interest-group model would predict.

The interest-group model suggests a political process that moves from interest group to policy. But in quite a number of important instances, this order is reversed. Policy precedes interest group, at least as the term interest group is commonly defined, as a number of somehow-organized persons pursuing some objective. The number of individuals and extent of organization among them required to warrant the label *interest group* is necessarily a matter of some dispute. Some brief examples of policymaking in which the expected sequence from interest group to policy is muddied may clarify the issue.

Alice Rivlin (1971) provides the first case, concerning policy debates on how to reform the welfare system that occurred in the mid- and late-1960s. Her account documents how the general perception, held largely by analysts and top-level federal administrators and apparently not advanced by any interest group outside of government, that something "should be done about" welfare, stimulated a series of analyses and debates that shaped perceived policy choices. As analysis progressed, perceptions of the problem shifted (for example, the problem of the aged poor looked less pressing as data on their assets were added to data on current income), and theories as to the causes of poverty shifted similarly (for example, the perverse influence of the then-existing welfare system in breaking up families emerged as an important cause of poverty). But the differences in policies advocated by the small number of individuals involved in this debate were often based not on differing analyses but on different basic values (for example, that it was or was not inherently demeaning to require an income test in order for a family to receive assistance for children). Differences were also based in different theories as to how Congress made decisions (that of building incrementally on existing program structures versus starting afresh), or on different theories as to how the general electorate would perceive (largely symbolically) a policy (such as suspicion that the electorate would believe a children's allowance program would be an incentive for the poor to have more children). Perceived budget constraints eliminated some alternatives (for example, a children's allowance without an income test). Rivlin concludes that analysis had considerable impact on policymaking in this case, but that analysts throughout felt inadequate because they had no "behavioral model of the population—at least of the low-income population—that would make it possible to simulate the effects of alternative policies" (Rivlin 1971, p. 32). Concluding her analysis of the shaping of perceptions of the causes of and possible responses to the poverty problem, an analysis almost totally based in theory building, Rivling argues for yet better theory on which to base policy.

Donald Schon's analysis of "the blindness system" provides a second example (1970). His analysis demonstrates how a theory as to the cause of blindness (accident or birth defect among otherwise healthy individuals) combines with values regarding self-sufficiency, leading to development of policies focused overwhelmingly on increasing the economic and physical self-sufficiency of blind individuals. Although available data on the incidence of blindness are woefully inadequate, and the highest estimate three times the lowest, all show that the proportion of potentially self-sufficient blind individuals is low. Theory and values in this case misdirected policy.

The third case concerns mental-health policy. James Cameron (1978) shows how reforms in the care of mentally-ill individuals (such as the shift from institutionalization to community-based care) occurred when two conditions were simultaneously present. A novel crisis had to require immediate action, and an ideology strongly held by some individuals central to policy-making had to be available to provide a *particular* policy alternative. He characterizes the process as essentially one of ideological warfare, requiring the legitimation of the new policy and systematic delegitimization of the existing policy. In the most recent such change in California, the crisis was a combination of increasing costs for state hospitals and legal and moral challenges to the institutionalization of individuals, especially without their consent or full legal procedures. The available alternative policy was community-based mental-health care, an ideology that Cameron (1978, p. 549) argues consisted of three interrelated claims: scientific respectability; moral righteousness; and economy. The power of the new ideology was such that plans were made to close all state hospitals, and resources were diverted to a community-based system. Large numbers of previously institutionalized patients were discharged with no administrative procedures available to link them to the new system. Cameron argues that the policy shift finally yielded service to a greatly expanded number of individuals, mostly those with moderate forms of mental distress, while more disturbed individuals fell out of the mental-health-care system (primarily into the welfare system in bed-and-care homes that have very limited therapeutic services, or into the justice system, where they might encounter a cycle of arrest and release until they were reinstitutionalized), at a total and per-unit-service cost much greater than that of the previous system.

In each of these cases, theory has had powerful impact on policy processes. Indeed, interest-group formation often follows rather than precedes policy. Welfare-rights organizations emerged in the 1960s, well after the basic structure of the welfare system was established. The number and membership of environmental-protection groups grew only after passage of the National Environmental Protection Act.

But the importance of theory in these cases pales compared with the importance of which economic theory dominates policymaking. Without the support and legitimization of a dominant economic theory that held that increased public-sector expenditures were a valid tool in managing the national economy, the explosion of programs and increase in public-sector spending that occurred in the 1960s through the mid–1970s could not have taken place. Barry Bosworth (1980) provides an excellent review of how national economic policymakers in the late 1970s sought to cope with inflation, slow productivity growth, and an uncertain energy supply, even as their confidence in Keynesian economic theory weakened. Because, among other reasons (including weak political institutions), that economic theory was not totally believed, policymaking tended to be unstable, weak, and frequently ineffective. Evidence of policy failures futher weakened belief in the theory. In the epilogue of a special issue of *The Public Interest* on "The Crisis in Economic Theory," Irving Kristol (1980) argues forcefully that all three identifiable economic schools now trying to construct a coherent, policy-relevant economic theory (neo-Keynesian, neo-Austrian, and Radical) are engaged in "rationalism." In short, the theories they are creating are social constructions most directly related to their images of what human society should be and their compulsion for rationally structured modes of discourse.

These examples suggest that theory building and policymaking are *processes,* each leading to social constructions, not to any immutable or "law-of-nature" products. As processes of social construction, theory building and policymaking share many attributes. Principal among these is their reliance on language.

This matter has been written about more self-consciously by those concerned with the philosophy of science than by students of policy. Jacob Brownowski writes persuasively and delightfully, advocating the position that science is not a special activity but rather "a type of all human activity" (1950, p. 113). As in all human activity, error plays a part, for neither individuals nor science can learn without errors. What emerges from this process of science is "a language for describing the world" (1950, p. 46). In some long-studied sciences, the language can take the form of precise laws, as is the case in astronomy.

Kaplan (1963) argues similarly that science is a process not unlike other human activity, intended to give understanding of our environs. Indeed, he defines theory most generally as a way of making sense out of a confusing situation. The process of discovery, of *doing* science, is governed by "logic-in-use," a cognitive style more or less rational, and the process of communication of understanding is governed by "reconstructed logic." A scientist may be socialized to employ a certain logic-in-use (in terms of interesting problems and likely causes), but logic-in-use is less confining, and may precede and be superior to reconstructed logics, which consist of more tightly circumscribed standards for acceptability. Reconstructed logics are especially important in communicating insight to others and in justifying (proving) the accuracy of insights. For Kaplan as for Brownowski, language plays a key role in the process of science.

The building blocks of any science are the development of concepts, the first level of abstraction. Concepts must have empirical elements and theoretical meaning to fulfill this role of bridging experience and theory. Concepts commonly order, classify, and analyze. Concept formation and theory formation go hand in hand. Brownowski offers the charming example of the people of a South Pacific island who have no concept of *tree,* instead giving each such plant a proper name. There can be no science of silviculture in such a society. In an example from social science, the concept of "income" has great usage among social scientists, policymakers, and the general population. It is most commonly given empirical meaning through definition as the equivalent of money received, but is open to ambiguity in measurement, such as when one speaks of "psychic" income. Theoretical usages of the term vary, including theories of social stratifications, potential for savings in a population, or social class. And each of the terms *social statification, savings,* and *social class* are themselves concepts. Theories are constructed of relationships among concepts.

Insights from this brief excursion into the philosophy of science can be translated into a model of policy processes. Policies are social constructions. Welfare, land-use, and strategic-deterrence policies all share this fundamental characteristic: they are social constructions. Ostrom would say they are artifacts "created by human beings with reference to the use of learning and knowledge to serve human purposes" (1980, p. 309). Just as science is built from concepts, so too is policy. And the concepts bear the same relationship to empirical phenomena and theory. The language of a policy process consists of ordering concepts (words) to achieve desired purposes. An advocate of community health care might characterize state hospitals as "inhumane institutions populated by individuals often committed there through procedures which violated constitutional rights." To act, policymakers must respond with words: words of statutes, regulations, or organizational and program design. To the extent policymakers seek to influence behavior not in single specified instances (such as, the Sheriff of Nottingham shall arrest Robin Hood) but in general (for example, officers shall enforce an anti-noise standard), as they must inevitably, the ambiguities and power of concepts and theories must be considered.

The language used in policy processes is not incidental or peripheral, it is of central importance. Probably one of the most powerful words used in the policy process is *right,* which commonly refers to individual behaviors such as the right to vote. A right is defined in our language as universal, inalienable, and uncompromisable. Small wonder that some of the most powerful public policies convey rights (such as the right to collective bargaining). Extension of the concept of rights from individual behaviors to receipt of services or certain statuses was one of the most important developments in public policymaking in the 1960s and 1970s. A new concept was developed to capture this new policy objective: *entitlement.* Because of their linkage to the concept of rights, entitlement programs (such as Food Stamps and Supplemental Security Income) are very difficult to reduce once launched. When expenditures in these programs exceed levels that policymakers find tolerable, they commonly resort to placing caps on the total expenditures available for the program. By this response, they avoid a policy debate for which they have virtually no vocabulary. For while it is possible to speak of an error rate, it is difficult to reduce coverage of the program or to terminate it altogether, because to do so is to take away rights, a linguistic logical impossibility. Whether or not it is a political im-

possibility is another matter; one which the current period of fiscal constraint is testing.

The entitlement example also illustrates the relationship between policies, theories, and values. Such policies are acceptable only in value systems
in which public responsibility for the welfare of individuals is acknowledged. And such policies are more plausible when the dominant economic
theory contains both explanation of why some individuals could be poor
(without resorting to personal-attitude or moral-behavior explanations) and
justification for high public-sector expenditures.

Several authors have explored the processes of change in theories and
language. John Dewey is one, holding that "knowledge is a function of
association and communication; it depends upon tradition, upon tools and
methods socially transmitted, developed and sanctioned . . . observation,
reflection and desire are habits acquired under the influence of culture and
institutions of society, not ready-made inherent powers . . . man acts from
crudely intelligized emotion and from habit rather than from rational consideration." (1927, p. 158). For Dewey, culture and institutions shape perceptions of what is and what can be; and habits of opinion are very per-
sistent, changing usually only after the events to which they are related
have changed. Thomas Kuhn (1962) argues similarly concerning change in
science, that most scientists engage in "normal" science according to some
paradigm that establishes important questions and acceptable methods of
inquiry. Paradigm changes are relatively rare, as in the replacement of New-
ton's mechanics with Einstein's theory of relativity. Paradigms do change,
however, usually when normal science cannot explain observed phenomena.
As science is a social construction, the process of paradigm change is re-
sisted by those committed to the previously dominant paradigm.

Lindblom and Cohen (1979) explore the relationship between social
science and problem solving. Action, that is, policymaking, is based mostly
on ordinary knowledge, the theories as to causes of behaviors and possibly
effective policies that are widely held in society. For example, policymaking
regarding juvenile delinquency may at one time be based on the theory that
all youths sow some wild oats and then shift to a theory that emphasizes the
disintegration of the nuclear family at another time. Social science (or professional social inquiry) is infrequently the basis of policymaking, becoming
usable only as it permeates ordinary knowledge. Schon's concept of "ideas
in good currency," is a related way of discussing the same phenomenon
(1971). His model of change involves an interplay between events such as
change in technology and those ideas in good currency, but the general
argument gives primacy to ideas in shaping the images of reality and possible policies in any given situation of policy choice.

Language and theory powerfully propel and constrain action. A major theme of this volume has been the exploration of how they contributed to the passage of Proposition 13 (and the larger phenomena of fiscal limits and fiscal constraint) and how they shape responses to those events. The responses to those events, it has been argued, will be of greater importance than the events themselves in shaping our society.

As a final illustration of this theme, consider the language and attendant theories and values of the increased fiscal assistance the state of California provided to local governments of that state after Proposition 13. Immediately after Proposition 13, state officials and most public discussants termed this assistance a "bail-out." Some local-government officials, especially from cities, recoiled at this language that suggested their errant behavior and dependency on the state. By 1979 (AB 8), the language had changed to "long-term fiscal assistance to local governments" (the official title of AB 8 was "long-term local government and school financing"). This language suggested the sharing of available revenues among governments, and the provision of the fiscal assistance in one bill emphasized the interdependence of all the governments in the state. By 1981, the language had changed again. Now the reference was increasingly of fiscal assistance to "local agencies" (Legislative Analyst 1981a, A–63). SB 102 (Chapter 101, Statutes of 1981), the bill affecting cities and what had previously been called "block grants" to counties, is written in terms of state subventions to local agencies. But what is a local agency? The word *agency* has little of the meaning of the word *government*. "Local agency" suggests subordination in policymaking to the state and emphasizes service delivery. "Local government" suggests sovereignty and functions in addition to service provision (such as conflict resolution or representation in the federal system). A knotty problem in our federal system, the nesting of legitimate representation and policymaking among levels of government, the higher ones of which are constitutionally superior to the lower, was submerged by this change in language. And the fragmentation of fiscal assistance into several bills implies that the issues involved can be fractured essentially according to the state's existing budget framework.

This shift in language reflects a real change in the way in which deliberations on fiscal assistance occurred. It reflects the growing domination of local governments by the state government of California. And it reflects the ascendance of the state legislature, whose needs in constructing an annual budget were satisfied by the changes. The value associated with this progression of language is that centralization is the appropriate response to fiscal constraint. The theory of political systems embodied in the progression is of a unitary rather than a federal system, and of technocrat-dominated service provision rather than political capacity as the purpose of government. These changes in language, in theory, and in action bode ill for the political system of California.

Bibliography

Advisory Commission on Intergovernmental Relations. 1980a. *Changing public attitudes on governments and taxes.* Washington, D.C.: ACIR.

———. 1976. *Improving urban America: A challenge to federalism.* Washington, D.C.: ACIR.

———. 1980b. *In brief: The federal role in the federal system: The dynamics of growth.* Washington, D.C.: ACIR.

———. 1980c. *Regional growth: Historic perspective.* Washington, D.C.: ACIR.

———. 1980d. *Significant features of fiscal federalism, 1979–1980.* Washington, D.C.: ACIR.

———. 1978. *State mandating of local expenditures.* Washington, D.C.: ACIR.

———. 1979. *States tackle tough fiscal issues. Intergovernmental Perspective* 5:6–30.

Agger, Robert et al. 1964. *The rulers and the ruled.* New York: Wiley.

Bacon, Kevin M. 1981. *City and county finances in the post-Proposition 13 era: An analysis of changes in the fiscal condition of California cities and counties during the 1977–78 to 1979–80 fiscal years.* 2 vols. Sacramento: Assembly Office of Research.

Beer, Samuel H. 1976. The adoption of general revenue sharing: A case study in public sector politics. *Public Policy* (Spring, 1976):127–195.

———. 1974. The modernization of American federalism. In *The Federal Polity,* ed. Daniel J. Elezar. New Brunswick, New Jersey: Transaction Books.

Bell, Daniel. 1974. *The coming of post-industrial society.* New York: Basic Books.

Biller, Robert P. 1976. On tolerating policy and organizational termination: Some design considerations. *Policy Sciencies* 7:133–149.

Boskin, Michael J. 1979. Some neglected economic factors behind recent tax and spending limitation movements. *National Tax Journal* 32: 37–42.

Bosworth, Barry P. 1980. Economic policy. In *Setting National Priorities: Agenda for the 1980s,* ed. Joseph A. Pechman, pp. 35–70. Washington, D.C.: Brookings Institution.

Braybrooke, David and Lindblom, Charles E. 1963. *A Strategy of Decision.* New York: Free Press.

Brownowski, Jacob. 1950. *The common sense of science.* Cambridge, Massachusetts: Harvard University Press.

137

Cameron, David. 1978. The expansion of the public economy: A comparative analysis. *American Political Science Review* 72:1243–1261.

Cameron, James M. 1978. Ideology and policy termination: Restructuring California's mental health system. *Public Policy* 26:531–570.

CBS. 1978. *California Primary Day Survey.* New York: CBS News.

Chaiken, Jan M. and Walker, Warren E. 1979. *Growth in municipal expenditures: A case study of Los Angeles.* Santa Monica: Rand Corporation.

Chapman, Jeffrey I. 1981. *Proposition 13 and land use: A case study of fiscal limits in California.* Lexington, Massachusetts: Lexington Books.

Chapman, Jeffrey I. and Kirlin, John J. 1979. Land use consequences of Proposition 13. *Southern California Law Review* 53:95–124.

Citrin, Jack. 1979. Do people want something for nothing: Public opinion on taxes and government spending. *National Tax Journal,* Supplement 32:113–130.

Clark, Terry N. and Ferguson, Lorna C. 1981. *Political processes and urban fiscal strain.* Unpublished paper, Department of Sociology, Univ. of Chicago.

Cochran, Nancy. 1980. Society as emergent and more than rational: An essay on the inappropriateness of program evaluation. *Policy Sciences* 12:113–130.

Coleman, James S. 1957. *Community conflict.* Glencoe, Illinois: Free Press.

Curry, R.L., Jr. and Wade, L.L. 1968. *A theory of political exchange: Economic reasoning in policy analysis.* Englewood Cliffs, New Jersey: Prentice-Hall.

Dewey, John. 1927. *The public and its problems.* Chicago: Swallow.

Doerr, David. 1979. The California legislature's response to Proposition 13. Cambridge, Massachusetts: paper presented at the Lincoln Institute of Land Policy.

Erie, Steven P. 1980. Public policy and black economic polarization. *Policy Analysis* 6:305–318.

Fitzgerald, Maureen S. 1980. Computer Democracy: An analysis of California's new love affair with the initiative process. *California Journal* 11:1–15.

———. 1979. The new Gann plan: Is it loaded with loopholes? *California Journal* 10:284–285.

Hamilton, Edward K. 1978a. On non-constitutional management of a constitutional problem. *Daedalus* 107:111–128.

———. 1978b. The greening of California: Notes on the politics of the Proposition 13 aftermath. Unpublished xerox, Los Angeles.

Hamilton, Edward K. and Rabinovitz, Francine F. 1977. *Whose ox will be healed? The financial effects of federalization of welfare.* New York: Ford Foundation.

Harris, Louis. 1978. Testimony before the Senate Subcommittee on Intergovernmental Relations. Unpublished xerox. Washington, D.C.: Louis
Harris and Associates.

Havemann, J. and Stanfield, R.L. 1977. A year later, the Frostbelt strikes
back. *National Journal* (July 2):1034–1037.

Heilbroner, Robert C. 1975. *The making of economic society.* Englewood
Cliffs, New Jersey: Prentice-Hall.

Huntington, Samuel. 1952. The Marasmuss of the I.C.C.: The Commission, the railroads and the public interest. *Yale Law Journal* 61:417–
508.

Jamison, Conrad. 1979. *California tax study.* Los Angeles: Security Pacific National Bank.

———. 1980. *California tax study: An analysis of revenue and expenditure of state and local government in California.* Los Angeles: Security
Pacific National Bank.

Janowitz, Morris. 1976. *Social control of the welfare state.* Chicago: Univ.
of Chicago Press.

Kammerer, Gladys, et al. 1963. *The urban political community.* Boston:
Houghton-Mifflin.

Kaplan, Abraham. 1963. *The conduct of inquiry: Methodology for behavioral science.* New York: Chandler/Harper and Row.

Kirlin, John J. 1979. Adapting the intergovernmental fiscal system to the
demands of an advanced economy. In *The Changing Structure of the
City* ed. Gary A. Tobin, vol. 16, Urban Affairs Annual Reviews. Beverly Hills, California: Sage Publications.

———. 1981a. *California's housing crisis: The consequences of policy failures?* Unpublished manuscipt. Sacramento: University of Southern
California, Sacramento Public Affairs Center.

———. 1975. Electoral conflict and democracy in cities. *Journal of Politics*
(February, 1975):262–269.

———. 1978. Principles and criteria for the allocation of functions among
government agencies. Task Force Project IV-2. Sacramento: Commission on Government Reform.

———. 1981b. The impacts of Proposition 13 upon the California political
system: Re-regulating the intergovernmental system. Paper presented
at the Conference on Political Economy, Carnegie-Mellon University,
May 1–2, 1981. Sacramento: Sacramento Public Affairs Center.

Kirlin, John J. and Chapman, Jeffrey I. 1980. Active approaches to local
government revenue generation. *The Urban Interest* 2:83–91.

Kristol, Irving. 1980. Rationalism in Economics. *The Public Interest,* Special issue, 1980), pp. 201–218.

Kuhn, Thomas. 1962. *The structure of scientific revolutions.* Chicago:
Univ. of Chicago Press.

Ladd, Everett. 1978. *Where have all the voters gone?* New York: W.W. Norton.

Landau, Martin. 1974. Federalism, redundancy and system reliability. In *The Federal Polity,* ed. Daniel J. Elezar. New Brunswick, New Jersey: Transaction Books.

LaPorte, Todd R. 1975. Complexity and uncertainty: Challenge to action. In *Organized social complexity,* ed. Todd R. LaPorte. Princeton, New Jersey: Princeton Univ. Press.

Leach, Richard H. and O'Rourke, Timothy G., eds. *Dimensions of state and urban policy making.* New York: Macmillan.

League of California Cities. 1980. *Cutback management, California style.* Sacramento: League of California Cities.

Levine, Charles H., Rubin, Irene S., and Wolohojian, George G. 1981. Fiscal stress and local government adaptations: Toward a multi-stage theory of retrenchment. College Park, Maryland: Bureau of Governmental Reseach.

Levine, Charles H. and Posner Paul L. 1979. The centralizing effects of austerity on the intergovernmental system. Paper presented at the 1979 Annual Meeting of the American Political Science Association, Washington, D.C.

Levine, Robert A. 1972. *Public planning: Failure and redirection.* New York: Basic Books.

Levy, Frank. 1979. On understanding Propostiton 13. *The Public Interest* 56:66–89.

Lilley, William, III and Miller, James C., III. 1977. The new 'Social Regulation' *The Public Interest* 47:49–61.

Lindberg, Leon et al. 1975. *Stress and contradiction in modern capitalism.* Lexington, Massachusetts: Lexington Books.

Lindblom, Charles E. 1977. *Politics and markets: The world's political-economic systems.* New York: Basic Books.

———. 1965. *The intelligence of democracy.* New York: Free Press.

Lindblom, Charles E. and Cohen, David K. 1979. *Usable knowledge: Social science and social problem solving.* New Haven, Connecticut: Yale Univ. Press.

Los Angeles Times. 1980a. *Los Angeles Times* poll. Los Angeles: Los Angeles Times, January 27, 1980: I.1.

———. 1980b. *Los Angeles Times* poll. Los Angeles: Los Angeles Times, May 11, 1980: I.1.

———. 1980c. *Los Angeles Times* poll. Los Angeles: Los Angeles Times, September 30, 1980: I.3.

Lovell, Catherine et al. 1979. *Federal and state mandating on local government: An exploration of issues and impacts.* Final Report to the National Science Foundation, Graduate School of Administration, Univ. of California, Riverside, California.

Lovell, Catherine and Tobin, Charles. 1981. The mandate issue. *Public Administration Review* 41:318–330.

Lowi, Theodore J. 1979. *The end of liberalism: The second rebublic of the United States,* second ed. New York: W.W. Norton.

McConnell, Grant. 1966. *Private power and American democracy.* New York: Vintage Books.

McDaniel, Linda. 1981. The message of Proposition 2-½. *Impact 2-½* 1:1.

Margolis, Larry. 1976. California legislature forfeits first place. In Eugene C. Lee and Larry L. Berg, *The challenge of California.* Boston: Little, Brown.

Nie, Norman, Verba, Sidney, and Petrocik, John R. 1976. *The changing American voter.* Cambridge: Harvard Univ. Press.

Olson, Mancur. 1977. The causes and quality of Southern economic growth. In: *The Economics of Southern Growth,* ed. E.G. Liner and L.K. Lynch. Research Triangle Park, North Carolina: Southern Growth Policies Board.

———. 1965. *The logic of collective action.* Cambridge, Massachusetts: Harvard Univ. Press.

Ostrom, Vincent. 1980. Artisanship and artifact. *Public Administration Review* 40:309–316.

———. 1979. *The intellectual crisis in American public administration.* Original edition. 1973. University, Alabama: Univ. of Alabama Press.

———. 1971. *The political economy of a compound republic: A reconstruction of the logical foundations of American democracy as presented in the Federalist.* Blacksburg, Virginia: Virginia Polytechnic Institute Center for Public Choice.

Owens, John R., Costantini, Edmond, and Weschler, Louis F. 1970. *California politics and parties.* New York: Macmillan.

Pascal, Anthony H. et al. 1979. *Fiscal containment of local and state government.* Santa Monica, California: Rand Corporation.

Pollard, Vic. 1981. Willie Brown, superstar. *California Journal* 12:128–130, 139.

Presthus, Robert. 1978. *The organizational society.* New York: St. Martin's.

Quinn, Tony. 1979. The proliferation of recalls in our single-issue society. *California Journal* 10:400–401.

Riles, Wilson. 1979. The delivery and financing of major intergovernmental programs (*Serrano* v. *Priest).* In State of California, Commission on Government Reform, *Final Report.* Sacramento: Commission on Government Reform.

Rivlin, Alice M. 1971. *Systematic thinking for social action.* Washington, D.C.: Brookings Institution.

Rodda, Albert S. 1980. *Supplement to January 15 paper on fiscal implications of Jarvis II on Proposition #9 as viewed from the perspective of a practical politician.* Sacramento, California: Senate Finance Committee (April 25, 1980).

Rosenthal, Alan and Forth, Rod. 1978. There ought to be a law! *State Government* 51:81–87.

Roth, William M. 1979. Supplementary views. *Final Report.* State of California, Commission on Government Reform. Sacramento: Commission on Government Reform.

Salzman, Ed. 1980. Ayatollah Campbell and the hostage budget. *California Journal* 11:326–327.

———. 1981a. The arms race. *California Journal* 12:287–295.

———. 1981b. Why they're cheering the "austerity" budget. *California Journal* 12:275–276.

Savas, E.S. 1977. Policy analysis for local government: Public vs. private refuse collection. *Policy Analysis* 3:2–26.

Schattschneider, E.E. 1960. *The semi-sovereign people.* New York: Holt-Rinehart and Winston.

Schlesinger, Arthur, Jr. 1981. Administration economics: End of illusions. *Wall Street Journal.* September 29, 1981. p. 26.

Schmitter, Phillipe C. and Lehmbruch, Gerhard, eds. 1979. *Trends toward corporatist intermediation.* Beverly Hills, California: Sage.

Schon, Donald A. 1971. *Beyond the stable state.* New York: Random House.

Schon, Donald A. 1970. The blindness system. *The Public Interest,* 18:25–38.

Schultze, Charles L. 1970. The role of incentives, penalties, and rewards in attaining effective policy. In *Public Expenditures and Policy Analysis,* ed. R. Haveman and J. Margolis. Chicago: Rand McNally.

Security-Pacific National Bank. 1980. *Economic report* (March, 1980) Los Angeles: SPNB.

Shalala, Donna E. 1980. Policy and research: A tough combination. *PS* (Spring, 1980):206–207.

Shannon, John. 1981. The great slowdown in state and local spending in the United States: 1976–1984. Washington, D.C.: Advisory Commission on Intergovernmental Relations.

Shefter, Martin. 1977. New York City's fiscal crisis: The politics of inflation and retrenchment. *The Public Interest* 48:95–127.

State of California, Auditor General, Joint Legislative Audit Committee. 1980. *Special districts: Opportunities for benefits through jurisdictional changes.* Sacramento: Office of the Auditor General.

State of California, Commission on Government Reform. 1979. *Final report.* Sacramento: Commission on Government Reform.

State of California, Council on Intergovernmental Relations. 1970. *Allocation of public service responsibilities in California.* Sacramento: California Council on Intergovernmental Relations.

State of California, Legislature. *California Legislature, 1977*. Sacramento: State of California Legislature, 1977.

State of California, Fair Political Practices Commission. 1980. *Campaign costs: How much have they increased and why?* Sacramento: FPCC.

———. 1981. *Sources of contributions to California state legislative candidates for the November 4, 1980 general election*. Sacramento: FPPC.

———. 1980b. *Two June ballot measures cost $4 million to qualify*. Sacramento: FPCC.

———. 1979. Proposition 4 spending over $1 million. Sacramento: FPCC.

State of California, Legislative Analyst, 1979. *An analysis of Proposition 4, the "Spirit of 13" initiative*. Sacramento: Legislative Analyst.

———. 1981a. *Analysis of the budget bill, fiscal year 1981–82*. Sacramento: Legislative Analyst.

———. 1981b. *Summary of legislative action on the budget bill, 1981–82 fiscal year*. Sacramento: Legislative Analyst.

State of California, Local Government Reform Task Force. 1974. *Public benefits from public choice*. Sacramento, California: Local Government Reform Task Force.

State of California, Office of Planning and Research. 1979. *New housing: Paying its way?* Sacramento: Office of Planning and Research.

———. 1980. *The growth revolt: Aftershock of Proposition 13?* Sacramento: Office of Planning and Research.

State of California, Secretary of State. 1979. *A history of the California initiative process*. Sacramento: Secretary of State.

State of California, State Controller. 1978. *Annual report of financial transactions concerning cities of California, fiscal year 1977–78*. Sacramento: State Controller.

Sundquist, James L. 1980. The crisis of competence in government. In *Setting national priorities: Agenda for the 1980's*, ed. Joseph A. Pechman. Washington, D.C.: Brookings Institution.

U.S., Bureau of the Census. 1957. *Government finances in 1956*. Washington, D.C.: U.S. Bureau of Census.

U.S., Office of Management and Budget. 1980. *Managing federal assistance in the 1980's*. Washington, D.C.: U.S. Office of Management and Budget.

———. 1979. *Special analyses of the budget of the United States, 1980*. Washington, D.C.: U.S. Office of Management and Budget.

Wildavsky, Aaron. 1979. *Speaking truth to power: The art and craft of policy analysis*. Boston: Little, Brown.

Wolin, Sheldon. 1968. *Politics and vision* Boston: Little, Brown.

Zimmerman, Joseph. 1973. Meeting service needs through intergovernmental service agreements. In *Municipal yearbook, 1973*. Washington, D.C.: International City Management Association.

Index

About the Author

John J. Kirlin is a professor of public administration at the Sacramento Public Affairs Center of the University of Southern California. In addition to several articles on Proposition 13, Professor Kirlin has written on metropolitan governance, alternative service-delivery structures, and the design of political institutions and policy strategies appropriate for a complex intergovernmental system. His consulting activities focus on policy and institutional design and the financing of land development and local government under conditions of fiscal constraint.